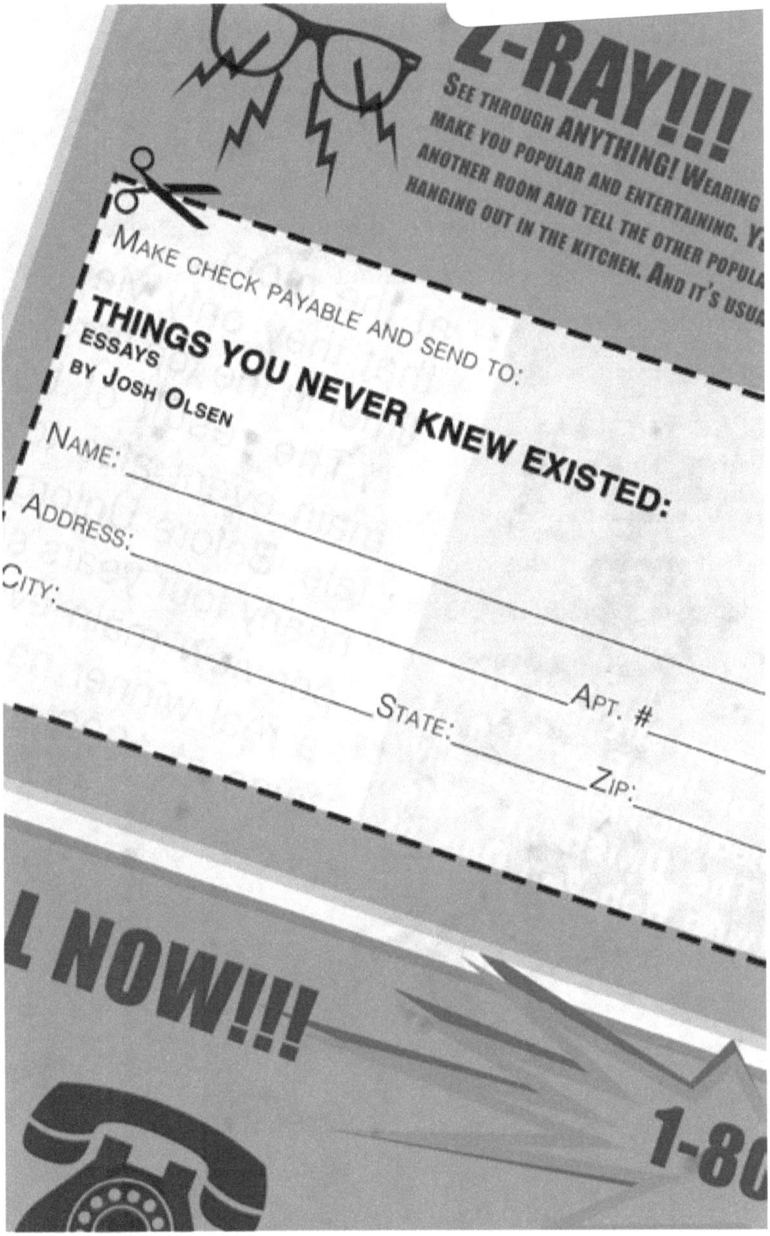
Z-RAY!!!
SEE THROUGH ANYTHING! WEARING
MAKE YOU POPULAR AND ENTERTAINING. Y
ANOTHER ROOM AND TELL THE OTHER POPULA
HANGING OUT IN THE KITCHEN. AND IT'S USUA
MAKE CHECK PAYABLE AND SEND TO:
THINGS YOU NEVER KNEW EXISTED:
ESSAYS
BY JOSH OLSEN
NAME:
ADDRESS:
APT. #
CITY:
STATE:
ZIP:
L NOW!!!
1-80

*Things You Never Knew Existed*
Copyright © Josh Olsen, 2024
ISBN: 979-8-9905466-1-5

This is a work of creative nonfiction. The events are portrayed to the best of Josh Olsen's memory. While all the stories in this book are true, some names and identifying details have been changed to protect the privacy of the people involved.

Cover Art: Doug Driesel Jr
Editor: Michele McDannold

Roadside Press
Colchester, Illinois

# Table of Contents

For Katie, Gabriella, Jackson, Kelso, and Archie

"You're the meaning in my life. You're the inspiration."
—Chicago, "You're the Inspiration"

# "The Hammer" Takes a Knee

Greg "The Hammer" Valentine takes a knee to sift through a box of action figures. It's possible that he's looking for one of himself (maybe even pocketing it while the vendor is away), and seeing how much it costs, compared to contemporaries Jake "The Snake" Roberts or Honky Tonk Man, but it's also possible that he's just feeling nostalgic. How odd it must be, that a ratty Rubbermaid container full of used rubber and plastic toys can substitute for a photo album or yearbook, the selection of action figures portraying the various stages and styles of your life and career, that manufacturers continue to distribute and profit off the likeness of deceased friends and relatives. I imagine that Valentine assumed that no one was watching him do this, or maybe he just didn't give a fuck. After all, what kind of yahoo would waste their time spying on Greg "The Hammer" Valentine as he looked through a box of gently used toys while a twenty-man over-the-top battle royal was taking place in the very same room? But most of the men presently in the squared circle have never had their very own action figure, and it's likely that most of them never will, and even though Greg "The Hammer" Valentine is now far from mint condition it isn't every day that you see a toy come to life.

# American Stepdad

My partner, Katie, once told me I was fortunate growing up, because lots of stepdads' beverage of choice is Wild Turkey, while my stepdad's was LaCroix sparkling water, but have you ever been screamed at by a sunburned, semipro golf player with raspberry LaCroix on his breath? That shit is terrifying.

My stepdad never hit me, but I feared him as though he did, and god have mercy on your soul if you drank his last cold Mtn Dew.

"Those are Steve's Oatmeal Creme Pies, but you can have a Little Debbie Nutty Bar" is something I used to say on the regular. "We have to be really, really quiet, Steve is watching *Star Trek: Next Generation*" is something else I used to have to say to friends if they visited while my stepdad was home and unemployed.

My stepdad was morally opposed to fishing and hunting, which he knew that my grandfather and I bonded over, but he always said that he wanted to buy a gun. He rarely talked politics, but he idolized Charles Bronson and Chuck Norris, angry white men who wouldn't hesitate to break the bones of young street tough stereotypes.

My stepdad wasn't a fighter, though. "Only fight someone if you can get away with it, and only hit someone where it won't leave a mark" is advice I received on more than one occasion.

I think my stepdad's greatest fear was being sued, although he would often threaten to sue at the drop of a hat, like a seasoned litigator, and yet he wouldn't hesitate to put the lives of others in serious danger.

My stepdad took great personal offense to any driver who dared pass him on the road. He'd swerve to cut them off then hit the gas, oftentimes forcing opposing commuters into a spontaneous game of chicken. When the offending driver would inevitably retreat, and then begin to honk and tailgate, my stepdad would slam on the brakes. He'd roll down his window, spit a massive wad of phlegm, give the other driver a stiff middle finger, and bludgeon them with a stream of obscenities like I've heard from few others since.

My stepdad introduced me to the words "motherfucker" and "cunt," but he used them sparingly, and with great intent.

In a way, you could say that my stepdad taught me the value of words. But he also taught me the value of Sergio Leone.

My stepdad was obsessed with Westerns and all things Clint Eastwood and fancied himself a bit of a modern-day cowboy.

Amid a trip to Wisconsin Dells, between the Ducks and Tommy Bartlett's Robot World, we stopped to take an old-fashioned family photograph, and Steve, of course, demanded the Western backdrop. He and my brother posed as a couple of gunslingers, my mother was dressed like a curvy saloon harlot (for lack of a better word), and I, the adopted one, was the "bandito," draped in an itchy wool poncho. When I recently found the lone surviving copy of this photograph in one of my mother's many photo albums, I read the inscription on the back, "Our one and only family vacation," and I laughed until I cried.

My stepdad played trumpet and taught himself how to play guitar. He could play acoustic versions of Loudon Wainwright III's "Dead Skunk" and Bryan Adams'"(Everything I Do) I Do It for You," which he employed to temporarily regain the affections of my mother.

For all intents and purposes, my stepdad disowned me when I was seventeen years old. He and my mother were embroiled in a nasty divorce, which only occurred after my mother birthed my two sisters, who were fathered by two different men who were not her husband. My brother remained in the custody of his father (my stepdad), while my mother raised her two young daughters, alone, in a studio apartment, and I moved in with my maternal grandparents. It was around this time that I received a handwritten letter from my stepdad, telling me goodbye, forever. I often think about my stepdad's letter, and I'll feel guilty for running away from him, but then I think about if I could ever do the same to my daughter, who's presently about the same age I was when I received my stepdad's letter, and I think to myself, fuck that dude.

I haven't spoken to my stepdad in about twenty years, but I did briefly see him, once, several years ago, when I was visiting home. Katie and I had stopped at the grocery store, to pick up some beer, and when I was exiting the parking lot I glanced in the rearview mirror and saw a familiar face. It was my stepdad, and he was riding a fucking motorcycle, instead of the broken-down station wagon or minivan he used to drive.

My thirty-three-year-old brother still lives with his father, and so even though I haven't communicated with him in roughly twenty years, I still know quite a bit about him, or at least I know what my brother tells me about him.

I know that he's an angry, miserable, and paranoid man. I know that he lives in darkness. I know that he leaves the dishes unwashed, for weeks at a time, and that he cooks by the greasy yellow light of the filthy microwave oven. I know that when he makes oven fries, he pours a layer of vegetable oil in the pan, and the kitchen fills with smoke as the oil spatters and burns. I know that he's still covetous of his Mtn Dew and Oatmeal Creme Pies. I know that he has a closet, which he padlocks, that is full of many of the childhood toys that I left in his house when I moved in with my grandparents, over twenty years ago.

I know that he has a practice putting green in the master bathroom.

My stepdad is a salesman, and, apparently, he's a good salesman. The website of the local appliance store that he works for, where he's worked for over two decades, is full of customer testimonials, thanking him for his excellent service and salesmanship. But he didn't always make his living selling flat-screen TVs and refrigerators. Over the span of his adult life, Steve served in the Air Force, but he also worked, early on, with computers, and did electronics repair. In the mid-80s, he attended night school, and earned a degree from the local technical college, but he also installed carpet and drywall, and later on spent a fair amount of time receiving unemployment, but not for a lack of desire to work. Sometimes the jobs just don't come, no matter how badly you want them, as I've come to know all too well, myself, and in the meanwhile, while you're waiting for the phone to ring, you might as well tear open a box of Oatmeal Creme Pies, crack an ice cold LaCroix, and enjoy a few episodes of M*A*S*H.

# Bennigan's

There's an elderly couple camped out in the parking lot of an abandoned Bennigan's.

Full-sized, luxury RV, Weber grill, folding chairs, red Coleman cooler.

These folks have options, and yet they chose to spread out in front of an empty restaurant that specialized in the Monte Cristo sandwich.

I hope to see them again someday, playing a vigorous game of badminton, adjacent to the condemned Pizza Hut, former home of the P'Zone.

# Meeting "Macho"

It's difficult to write about a memory you can't remember. For the past several years, I'd say ever since the untimely death of "Macho Man" Randy Savage, on May 20, 2011, I've been trying to recall the night that I attended a live taping of WCW Thunder, in my hometown of La-Crosse, Wisconsin, but every time I do, I draw a blank. Thanks to the internet and the help of a few friends, I've been able to narrow down the date to August 5, 1999, but even still, when I read and reread the various online dirtsheets and results listings, it reads as totally unfamiliar, and I can't say with absolute certainty that was indeed the night in question. I simply can't remember any of it. Well, with the exception of a few details.

I specifically remember my wardrobe that day. I was sporting a crisp new pair of black denim Sean Jean brand overalls and a black t-shirt. I feel like I only remember this because my friend Barry, who was visiting from Houston, Texas, and with whom I attended the live event, had mocked me for unintentionally dressing like a "less than buff" Buff Bagwell (who was on the card that night). And the other main thing I remember from that night is that when Barry and I entered the LaCrosse Center Box Office, to purchase our tickets mere hours before the show, we actually met Macho Man Randy Savage. He was simply walking around inside the empty LaCrosse Center lobby, not unlike Barry and myself, except Barry and I were a couple of stoned young men, looking to waste a little free time before the big show, and Macho Man was arguably the greatest professional wrestler to ever live.

I'll willingly admit that I was completely starstruck. I couldn't do anything but wordlessly stare at Macho Man, who was jacked to the gills yet surprisingly short, but Barry jumped into action without hesitation, immediately grabbing the attention of Macho Man and shaking his hand. Barry remembered that I had a disposable camera in the pocket of my overalls, as I often did back then, and he and Macho Man posed with their fists interlocked. I snapped the picture, Barry enthusiastically thanked Macho Man, and I also silently shook his hand as he walked by. In the years since, I've had the pleasure of meeting and shaking the hands of many other professional wrestlers, a number of whom I would consider among the greatest to practice the craft, but due to the serendipitous nature under which I met the Macho Man, no other wrestler meet-and-greet has felt so momentous.

When I've talked to Barry about that night, and what he remembers about it, he also can't seem to remember a single thing, other than meeting Macho Man (and maybe my glorious Sean Jean overalls), and he's joked that it feels like the magic of meeting Macho Man before the show is somehow responsible for erasing our memory of the remainder of the night, and I've started to agree with him. It was such a wholly unexpected surprise that meeting Macho Man was destined to overshadow anything else that occurred. Of course, for myself, there were probably other factors also involved in my lack of retention. If, in fact, the date of that particular WCW Thunder is correct, and we were there on August 5, 1999, that means that it had been a little over four months since my first child was born on March 22, 1999. I was barely twenty years old, and I was consumed with the stress and emotion of being a new parent, so perhaps that's one reason why the only thing I remember is meeting Macho Man.

With that said, this was one of those rare occasions, before smartphones and social media, in which there actually exists, or existed, documentation of the night's events. For starters, I had a disposable camera, and I had used it throughout the night, first by taking a picture of Barry and Macho Man, and I can assume I took pictures throughout the night, but as it so happens, the film in that camera never got developed. Like much of the film I used from around that time, I simply threw it into a dresser drawer or shoebox and forgot about it. A number of years later, I made it a point to eventually attempt to develop my saved rolls of film, but I quickly found out that much of the film just wasn't worth developing. Most of the film had simply expired, which I didn't then know could happen. And so, I finally made the decision to indiscriminately throw away all of my saved, undeveloped film. Now, in doing so, did I also throw out a great number of wonderful memories, photographs of my friends and family and infant daughter? Did I also throw out my undeveloped photograph of Barry shaking hands with Macho Man Randy Savage? I did. I threw it all away. But at the time, I decided it just wasn't worth trying to develop a box full of unlabeled, indistinct, and expired rolls of film, in the off chance that I might finally uncover those missing pictures from WCW Thunder, when there was an equal or better chance that when I went to the CVS photo lab I'd be stuck paying for a thick envelope full of glossy 4X6 photos of indistinguishable exposures. So, that eliminated part of the evidence of what Barry and I saw and experienced that night. That further distanced the memory, and any chance of recovering it.

And yet, this was a televised event. This was an episode of WCW Thunder, and hence, it is something I could actually watch, if I could only find it. (this was before the WWE Network) As it turns out, the episode of WCW Thunder that Barry and I attended was a two-parter. There was the live portion, which aired on Thursday, August 5, and then there was the taped portion, which aired on Thursday, August 12, 1999. So far, I've been unable to locate any video of the live August 5th episode of WCW Thunder, just a collection of results and summaries, with the occasional screenshot thrown in to add some color, but one of the screenshots I've found at least looks familiar. In it, Macho Man Randy Savage is being interviewed, in ring, by "Mean Gene" Okerlund, and I swear that Macho Man is wearing what he was wearing when Barry and I met him in the LaCrosse

Center, before the show. Rather than his ring gear, Macho Man is wearing a black, sequined, collared shirt, black leather pants, black sunglasses, and black leather Kangol-style hat. Granted, this was the general style of Macho Man around that time, well after the brightly colored robes and fringed jackets and cowboy hats, well after "Pomp and Circumstance," Miss Elizabeth, Slim Jims, and ICOPRO. But this image of Macho Man, and what he was wearing, his street clothes, felt too familiar to be a coincidence.

Still, that one image wasn't enough to fully convince me that Barry and I were at WCW Thunder, and hence met Macho Man, on August 5, 1999, and so I kept searching. And while I never found any video from the August 5th episode, I did come upon the full episode of the August 12th edition of WCW Thunder, which was taped on August 5. So, this was it, at last, video evidence of that night, assuming that I could remember any of it. It was very possible that the entire episode would seem completely foreign to me. I wasn't a diehard WCW Thunder viewer back then, and so at least my viewing memory wouldn't skew what might've been the wrong episode. Therefore, I concluded that if I could recall anything from this particular episode of WCW Thunder, then that would finally help fill in the blank, as far as what occurred that night, and most importantly, help nail down the actual date of when Barry and I met Macho Man Randy Savage.

I'm not going to run down the entire episode, because the point here isn't to write a review. If you want to know exactly what happened on the August 12th episode of WCW Thunder, back in 1999, there's no shortage of information available. You can even watch the episode, yourself, if you can find it (spoiler alert: Rick Steiner defeats Spyder and Sid Vicious defeats the tag team of Disorderly Conduct). The important thing is, for about the first half of the video, I felt completely dismayed. Nothing about this episode, in any way, felt like I had been there or seen what was happening in the ring. Part of the issue was that this was the "go home" episode of WCW Thunder, before the 1999 Road Wild pay-per-view, and so most of the televised episode was spent recapping the previous week's episode of WCW Monday Nitro, and reminding viewers of the various feuds and matches heading into the upcoming event in Sturgis, South Dakota, but the little that actually did occur in the ring felt previously unseen. Therefore, I conceded that this was the wrong episode, and that Barry and I hadn't been at WCW Thunder on August 5, 1999.

It was disappointing, feeling so close to rewatching a forgotten memory, and then realizing that the memory wasn't yours in the first place. And so, convinced that I had come to a dead end in my research, I continued to halfheartedly watch the rest of the August 12th episode of WCW Thunder, but my attention began to stray from the action in-ring. I began to search the crowd for familiar faces. Barry and I had known a number of other people who were at that same event, and so I tried to identify somebody, anybody, I knew. And more so than that, I was trying to find myself and Barry. That night, we were sitting in the lower bowl section of the LaCrosse Center, in seats facing what's referred to as the hard camera, and I hoped that I might see myself on TV. There were a number of moments when I thought I caught a glimpse of either myself or Barry, but then something, some sign or odd piece of clothing or merch, would almost immediately disprove that it was us.

At one point in the video, a man in the audience suddenly stands and raises a camera to his eye, and a part of me felt this might have been me. He had similarly styled dark hair and an unfortunate beard (did I have a beard then?), similar black t-shirt and a camera in hand, but then again, the likelihood seemed too coincidental for my taste. I rewatched this brief moment at least five more times, if not more, but I ultimately decided that it was somebody else. And then, at a little over one hour into the video, after a brief clip of a confrontation between Dennis Rodman and Macho Man Randy Savage that occurred on an episode of *The Tonight Show* with Jay Leno, the episode cut back to the LaCrosse Center, where Macho Man was headed into the ring to face young Evan Karagias (pronounced like "courageous"), and I suddenly remembered, Macho Man made two appearances that night. There was the earlier in-ring interview with Mean Gene, which aired live on August 5, 1999, but then there was the actual match Macho Man had later that same night, which served as the main event of the evening.

Macho Man was wearing the same wardrobe that he wore during his interview with Mean Gene, which was the same wardrobe he was wearing, preshow, when Barry and I met him in the empty LaCrosse Center lobby. I vividly remembered the motions of Macho Man's match with Karagias. The out-of-context pre-match promo about a Hummer, Macho Man shaking Karagias' hand and then kicking him in the gut, the involvement of Macho Man's forgettable blond valet, who was a lackluster substitute for Miss Elizabeth. There was no doubt in my mind, I had seen this all before. I was there that night.

By the time the match reached its inevitable conclusion, and Macho Man dropped a total of three flying elbows upon a supine Evan Karagias, I had fully made up my mind. It was settled, Barry and I attended WCW Thunder, and thus met Macho Man Randy Savage, on August 5, 1999. It was satisfying to finally have a definitive date attached to this memory. There was never any doubt that Barry and I met Macho Man, yet it ragged on me that I could remember so little about that night, let alone when, exactly, it had happened. But once I watched, or technically rewatched, Macho Man Randy Savage's otherwise forgettable squash match against Evan Karagias, my memory was replenished. At last, I could finally stop obsessing over what I couldn't remember about that night, and instead, I could cherish the irreplaceable memory of what happened that day.

# Spontaneous

Katie recently told me that she can tell I was most-ly raised by my grandparents. She called me the oldest young person she knows. Or was it the youngest old person? Either way, her point was made. And I can't deny it, as much as I'd like to try. I do appreciate a quiet night at home, devoid of surprise run-ins or unsched-uled interruptions. Even when I make plans, well in ad-vance, no matter how much I'm looking forward to it, whether it's a concert, a baseball game, a poetry reading, or a live pro wrestling event, when the day of the show comes, I'd rather stay at home, and even after I've con-vinced myself to go, no matter how much I enjoy it in the moment, I'm happiest when it's over. Katie told me that I lack spontaneity, and my response was that I expe-rienced enough spontaneity in my childhood to last me the rest of my life. Katie rightfully groaned and rolled her eyes, her response whenever she felt I was playing the victim, and I said, "I lived in twenty different houses before I was sixteen!" My mom and my stepdad were spontaneous, spontaneous with their jobs and their bills and their fidelity and rent, and as a result of their spon-taneity, we would spontaneously move to two or three different apartments in one year. During the first grade, I attended three different elementary schools (one of them twice that year), a fact that still makes my mother cry when I bring it up. All three schools were within the same school district, in Holmen, Wisconsin, a village with fewer than 10,000 people, but for a first grader in the mid-1980s, they might as well have been on different continents. For one of the schools, I was only enrolled a couple weeks, while I temporarily lived with my grandparents (hardly the first or last time). I barely remember anything about it, except for pissing my pants one day because I was too shy to raise my hand and ask for permission to be excused for the boy's room, but it turns out that my brief presence evolved into a bit of an urban legend for my classmates. One evening, in my early twenties, I was approached by a group of drunk college students (granted, I was also then a drunk college student) and asked if my name was "Josh Sather." And, well, the answer was yes. "Sather" was my legal last name before I was adopted by my stepdad, when I was in the second grade, but for these strangers to know me by that name, it meant they would've had to know me before then. So, yeah, I was Josh Sather, I confessed, and my answer was met with an explosion of laughter and profanity. "Holy shit, where the fuck did you go?" one of them asked. "What the fuck happened to you?" another slurred. "I told you he existed!" said another. As it turns out, this gathering of intoxicated individuals had all gone to school together, from kindergarten through senior year of high school, and my two weeks in their classroom, in first grade, was like a blip in their collective memory, like a shared delusion. The weird, quiet, ambiguously ethnic apparition who showed up, unannounced, in the middle of the school year, and then vanished without a trace, just a couple weeks later. *Did that even happen?* they'd joke amongst themselves, *Was he even real?* And finally, it was confirmed, like the existence of Bigfoot. Josh Sather lived! "And that," I proclaimed, "was the result of spontaneity." Katie just looked at me and yawned, and then so did I.

## Everything Zen

We crossed the state line into Beloit, Wisconsin, passing that towering silo of steaming Hormel chili.

My daughter stuffed her face with a handful of cannabis-oil-infused potato chips.

"We've got *Bush*!" the rock-jock on our Ford's FM radio exclaimed over the opening strains of "Everything Zen."

# Rock Me, Roll Me, Jackyl Me Off!

I recently attended my very first Jackyl concert, and I can say with almost 100% certainty that it will also be my last.

I could lie and pretend that I wasn't on my feet, drunkenly cheering and dancing as Jesse James Dupree, lead vocalist for Jackyl, chainsawed a perfectly functional wood stool, but I was, and it felt damn good to do so.

It was easily one of the dumbest things I'd ever seen, but the sheer spectacle of the seemingly mindless destruction, on Dupree's behalf, was unlike few things I'd witnessed before.

With little effort, I could make the claim, based upon legitimately objective criteria, that this was the worst concert I have ever attended, but if I were to do so, I feel as though that would nullify how great of a time I actually had, laughing my ass off, throughout the duration of the night.

Now, please allow me to make myself perfectly clear, my intention here is not to mock the band Jackyl.

After all, I honestly feel as if that is impossible to do.

Jackyl is exempt from criticism.

There is no way to effectively critique a band whose most celebrated tune, "The Lumberjack," features a chainsaw solo, and as a matter of opinion, I would have to admit that Jackyl's musical history, if anything, is actually quite admirable.

Before the night of the show, I had absolutely no idea that Jackyl had any more than one album, their 1992 platinum-selling, self-titled debut, and so my assumption was that their concert would consist of a quick run through of their greatest hits, a relatively concise list, including their highest charting single, "Down on Me," then cap off the evening with a stirring rendition of "The Lumberjack," and call it a night.

But by no means, whatsoever, was this a nostalgia tour.

Jackyl was not out to wallow in their early 90s success.

They had a new album to promote, their eleventh to

date, and Dupree had bottles of his very own "America's Outlaw Bourbon Whiskey" to shill.

Jackyl is clearly a band that time, and most of society, has forgotten, but they continue to work and record and tour, and you wouldn't have known that Jackyl was not firmly situated on top of the Billboard Charts based upon the majority of men and women in attendance on the night of Jackyl's triumphant return to LaCrosse, Wisconsin.

The audience was not comprised of casual Jackyl fans, these were devotees, thoroughly clad in a wide array of Jackyl-inspired attire (typically a sleeveless concert t-shirt tucked into pleated jeans), and their enthusiasm was genuinely contagious.

Of the nearly two-hour long set list, I was familiar with exactly two songs, both from their twenty-year-old debut album, not counting the occasional cover tune, but it seemed as though the entirety of the crowd was fluent in Jackyl.

Even when Dupree and crew introduced the occasional

new single, the audience responded with heartfelt excitement, and was quick to learn and sing along to the generally simplistic hook, such as, "She make the booty go boom, boom, boom!"

And at the end of Jackyl's two-hour set, when it was finally time for the band to depart the stage, a lucky fan who had won a local radio contest was granted the opportunity to carry forth the sacrificial stool.

Dupree revved his chainsaw, the band kicked into the opening riff of "The Lumberjack," and the crowd erupted into a near hysterical scream of elation.

This is what I had paid for, to see a grown man chainsaw a wood stool.

Suddenly, all the glaring shortcomings of the concert—the tinny sound quality, the heat and mosquitoes, the bar consisting exclusively of canned Miller products (with the striking exception of High Life), and, honestly, the mediocre hard rock music—were laid to waste in Jackyl's sawdust.

Was it worth the cost of a $25 ticket?

Honestly, probably not.

And will I ever go to another Jackyl concert?

No, once was more than enough.

But, for that one night, it was liberating to be part of an absolutely irony-free crowd—save for, perhaps, myself—and scream out from the bottom of my soul, "Rock Me, Roll Me, Jackyl Me Off!"

# Relisted

For the third time in as many months, I received an automated email from eBay, stating, "An item you've been watching has been relisted." The item in question is a Toxic Avenger vending machine prism sticker, and it's one of the most beautiful pieces of ephemera I've ever seen, but it comes with a price tag of $200, and so I'll keep on watching it, and rewatching it, until someone clicks the blue "Buy It Now" button and removes it from my purview. The individual attempting to sell the Toxic Avenger sticker is a vendor who goes by the name steventiques. According to his seller profile page, steventique's "main passion is Early American Pattern Glass," which comprises the majority of the items he has for sale, but he also lists a rather impressive number of late 80s-early 90s vending machine stickers, including a selection of extremely rare Selectra brand prism stickers, of which the Toxic Avenger sticker is the most expensive sticker listed. Other Selectra vending machine prism stickers for sale in steventique's eBay store feature widely known horror characters, such as Jason Voorhies, Leatherface, and Freddy Krueger, as well as stickers from cult favorites like *Sleepaway Camp III*, *Shocker*,

*Swamp Thing* (another personal favorite), and *Night of the Demons*, in addition to the aforementioned Toxic Avenger. It wasn't that long ago that I had absolutely no idea, whatsoever, that any of these stickers existed, but now that I know, it's become a minor obsession, and in addition to that, I've become mildly obsessed with the vendor, steventiques, as well. Steventiques' items ship from Kenosha, Wisconsin, so it's probably safe to assume that is where he lives. His profile states that he is "interested in the preservation, education, and history of American glassmaking," but then why is he selling so many of these prism stickers, and how did he procure them? The description under each sticker states, "I have found a few Horror Prism Vending Stickers in an old warehouse," and I'm immediately jealous. This makes me want to move back to Wisconsin, to small-town, rural Wisconsin, where fewer people feel motivated to go scavenging around in abandoned warehouses full of undiscovered treasure. I currently own two vintage vending machine prism stickers. One showcases David Cronenberg's horror/sci-fi classic, *Scanners*, from the highly sought collection of rare Selectra horror stickers, and the other is a prism sticker which features an image of a kneeling, blond, bikini-clad woman, adjacent to the admittedly sexist caption *GIRLS WANTED: No Experience Needed*. I purchased both of these stickers from a vendor at a Metro Detroit-area pop culture convention, Motor City Nightmares, for $10 a piece. In the moment, I recall thinking that perhaps I was being overcharged, but this was before I had learned about the rarity of these stickers, and well before I stumbled across steventiques, and his enviable collection of vending machine prism stickers. The few other *Scanners* stickers I've seen for sale online have typically listed for about $15 each, and I'm yet to find another copy of the *GIRLS WANTED* sticker I purchased; therefore, I've concluded that what I paid was more than fair. My only regret is that I didn't buy more when I had the chance. Who knows if I'll ever see that same vendor, with his tacklebox full of vending machine stickers which once sold for fifty cents apiece in arcades and bowling alleys and gas stations and hotel lobbies, ever again? So, in the meanwhile, I've got eBay, and I've got steventiques, and steventiques' got a $200 Toxic Avenger vending machine prism sticker. I recently found a second Toxic Avenger prism sticker on eBay, and this one is selling for half the price. For $99.99, I could finally own the Toxic Avenger prism sticker that I've been watching, and rewatching, as it's repeatedly relisted, since April 2016. But this one doesn't seem as crisp as steventiques'. Maybe it's just a lack of skill on the part of the photographer, but the prism doesn't look nearly as sharp, and Toxie's visage looks a little washed-out. If you ask me, it's clearly a subpar example of an otherwise extraordinary sticker, and not worth the $99.99, no matter the rarity of the specimen. So, rather than waste money I don't have on a lackluster copy, I'd rather continue to fawn over the real deal. And besides, even if I can't afford Toxie, I can buy steventiques' glorious Swamp Thing sticker for less than $15.

# Watch Out!

Troy W. asks a lot of questions, and he talks a little bit too much, but he cautiously avoids pertinent details that relate to his identity. He seems overly eager and rushed. It is obvious what he's doing, but I want to give him the benefit of the doubt. I don't want to believe that he's trying to rip me off, even though I'm more than aware that is exactly what he's doing. My job would be much easier if I could just be honest with these petty con artists, but I can do little more than make passive attempts at intercepting Troy's goal of walking out the door with an armful of merchandise, essentially for free, with little-to-no real consequence.

To summarize, I manage a chain video store, and Troy is creating a new customer account, with the intention of renting out multiple brand-new video games, while spending as little money as possible, only to never bring them back. I'd like to say this is an isolated incident, but frustratingly, it is not. The video store I presently manage (or assistant manage) is located in a rather quiet, suburban neighborhood, west of Detroit, so we don't get these scammers on a daily basis, but my inbox is full of emails sent from the managers and employees of nearby locations who get hit multiple times each week.

The subject line of the emails read *WATCH OUT!!!* or *KEEP YOUR EYES OPEN!!* or some other melodramatic, all-caps warning, and the body of the messages contain more or less the same narrative. So-and-so is jumping from store to store, setting up multiple new accounts, and taking as many video games as they possibly can. If they're quick enough, and if they aren't already flagged in the POS (point of sale) system, these ambitious schemers can sometimes hit multiple stores in one day, and get away with hundreds of dollars of merchandise, before the company takes notice. But even that sometimes won't stop them. They'll use assumed identities, or the ID cards of friends and family. They'll often bring a spouse or girlfriend or cousin or even a parent or adult child along, so if their name or number is already associated with a banned account, they'll have their associate open an account in their name instead. But sometimes they'll exhaust all their options, and they'll spend the day calling every store in the district, asking if they can check the balance on their account. And if their account has been suspended, they'll ask to check another account, and then another, and then they'll hang up and call back an hour later, from another phone number, or a blocked line, and ask to check on another account, all while pretending that you haven't already spoken to them three times earlier that day, and while you pretend that you haven't already received multiple emails and phone calls from other store managers and employees, warning you that these phone calls are about to come. The customer pretends that he isn't a con man, and you, the employee, the customer service representative, have to pretend that you don't know this customer is a petty criminal.

Then again, perhaps I should refrain from labeling them as criminals. The legality (or illegality) of what the customer has done, or is attempting to do, falls into a somewhat gray area. They aren't exactly stealing. It's not like they're shoplifting. They're not sneaking through the exit with a video game hidden under their jacket. They are paying the amount of money the cashier is requiring them to pay. However, they are breaching a contract, an agreement that they will return the merchandise they are renting, when that was never the customer's intention, in the first place. And what is the consequence of this breach of contract? Well, basically nothing. So, can we call this action a crime, if there is no legal penalty? Sure, the offending customer might get a few annoying phone calls, if the phone number they gave isn't disconnected or a wrong number, and we didn't call to verify it first, but there is no larger ramification, other than the inconvenience of having to procure their video games and/or movies from another location, or by the means of another customer's identity. We have the customer's name, address, phone number, and driver's license/ID number, but we make no effort to collect what is owed to us. Many years ago, I had a significant other who, along with her roommate, furnished their apartment with the assistance of a local rent-to-own business. It wasn't long before they decided to stop paying the monthly rental costs, and so the rent-to-own store repossessed their furniture. When a library loans a patron a book, it is agreed upon that the book will be returned to the library, or there will be a penalty. In the case of an academic library, if a book is not returned, and the patron does not pay for the item to be replaced, the patron's transcripts may be suspended, or they may not be allowed to register for the next term's courses, or they might not be allowed to graduate. In the case of a public library, the patron may receive a bill, and even be sent to collections. But we, at the video store for which I work, do none of this. No legal action, no bills, no collection agencies, no debt collectors. All we can presently do is attempt to stop these customers from walking away with any more of our merchandise once we've been burned. It's a "fool me once" system, with the burden of accountability laid firmly upon the shoulders of the employee, and I've been fooled my fair share of times.

It doesn't make me angry, but it's frustrating, and it's exhausting, dealing with these small-time hustlers, and trying to keep our merchandise out of their hands, but they're so determined, and they're so ambitious in their attempts to deceive us, that it's almost impressive. These aren't juvenile delinquents, these are grown men (almost always men), with the time and resources to spend a considerable part of their day calling around and driving from city to city, store to store, in order to walk away with a couple previously played, out-of-box video games, and it's almost always video games they want. After all, movies are easy to pirate, and there's no resale value to DVDs. Video games, however, are relatively high-dollar, high-demand items. Even used games can hold much of their retail value, and in rare instances, even surpass their original price tag. But what do these customers want with these video games they acquire? I'm sure that many of them actually play them, or give them to their kids and friends to play, but if they simply wanted to play the game, why wouldn't they just rent one, return it, then rent another, like most customers do? Why are they willing to create multiple accounts, and dummy accounts, at multiple stores? Why are they willing to tarnish their identity, and possibly the identities of their friends and family members?

The day after I created Troy W.'s new account and allowed him to walk out the door with three video games (two Xbox One and one PlayStation 4), to the tune of $4.50 (thanks to the new member ½ off discount), I received a phone call from an employee at a store located in Taylor, Michigan. The employee on the other end of the line was calling to verify an account from our store, and sure enough the account in question belonged to Troy W. He was attempting to open another new account, at a store roughly thirty minutes south of us. When I told the woman on the phone that his account at my store was less than twenty-four hours old, and that he still retained the video games he had rented from me, two of which he was trying to rent duplicates of in Taylor, the cashier from the other store politely informed Troy W. that he would not be allowed to open a new account, to which I overheard the voice of another male customer reply, "Fuck it, lemme open one then." Shortly after, our brief phone exchange came to an end, and I immediately turned to the nearest computer, and began to type an email addressed to all of the stores in my district, with a subject line that read, *Watch Out!*

# Exquisite

"**O**h God," the man choked, sounding like he might vomit. "Oh God, what did I do?" What he had done was spend $450 on a single pack of football cards and got completely skunked. Clearly, this was money the man did not have to freely spend, on football cards or anything else, but regardless of that, he had confidently burst into the store, dressed for what looked to be custodial work, shoved his way through the modest crowd of customers gathered around the glass case of sports cards and memorabilia, and handed a personal check to the man at the register. In exchange, the man at the register retrieved a small, green-and-gold shrink-wrapped cardboard box. And the rest, as they say, is history. It doesn't matter who or what the man got in this pack of five football cards. Whatever he got, it didn't justify the $450 price tag. "Pathetic," the man seethed through clenched teeth, his pitiful loot spread out before him, "motherfucking pathetic." He raised his tightly balled fists to his temples, the muscles in his toned forearms flexing and twitching, and then suddenly pantomimed like he was slamming them down onto the glass display case below. Nearly everyone in the store flinched and gasped, and the man at the register, the man who had sold the pack of cards, wisely remained quiet, even though he looked as though he was trying to think of how to ask his customer, a very loyal and well-paying customer, to leave and not come back, but before anyone had the chance to properly react, the man jammed his hands in his pockets, gave a bitter little laugh, and walked out the door. Once he was gone, and the air of near intolerable tension dissolved, the remaining customers breathed an audible sigh of relief and went back to business as usual, flipping through binders and ripping open packs of cards and wheeling and dealing with the now overly friendly man at the register, but barely more than a few minutes passed before the disgruntled customer made his unexpected, and wholly undesired, return. In the flurry of his sudden departure, he'd accidentally left behind his recent purchase—skunked or not, he'd be taking it home— and since he had to come all the way back, what the hell, he dryly reasoned with his checkbook in hand, he'd take one more pack of those fucking cards.

# Things You Never Knew Existed

While flipping through a stack of early 90s Marvel comic books, issue 25 of *The New Warriors*, to be exact, I came upon a full-page ad for "Things You Never Knew Existed…," but the beauty of it was, they were all things you definitely knew existed. On an individual basis, these things were all pretty unextraordinary, things like sea monkeys, baseball cards, a rubber snake, and a *Star Trek Next Generation* pin, but taken as a whole, it painted a rather disturbing portrait. It read like a one-stop shop for aspiring psychopaths. Sure, customers could order harmless novelty items like smoking golf balls and snapping "ouch" gum, but you could also fill your basket with police badges, chrome-plated handcuffs, and a laminated private investigator card. There's a spy book camera, super listener, pocket spy telescope, and spy sunglasses. You could learn to hypnotize yourself and others. There's even a diver's knife. And for when you needed to make it weird, they even had leather fingerless gloves. The company who placed the ad, the Johnson Smith Company, was based out of Florida, and I was surprised to learn that they're still in operation, but rather than placing ads in comic books, they now have a website, titled what else but *Things You Never Knew Existed*.... The Johnson Smith Company still sells hokey junk like gag lotto tickets and fart extinguishers, but they're also an online source for books and DVDs about the illuminati and the new world order, as well as the male g-spot. Their best sellers are a Donald Trump coffee mug that reads "Finally Someone With Balls" and a t-shirt that reads "The 10 Commandments Are Not Multiple Choice!" and suddenly their fake vomit and poop soap don't seem quite so funny.

*

For a short period of time, my brother and I sold cheap stationery and Christmas cards for the Olympic Sales Club. The colorful ad reproduced en masse in the pages of comic books and *Boys' Life Magazine* boasted cash and prizes, and the free catalog featured items like keyboards (twenty-six items) and jukeboxes (fifty-five items) and BMX bikes (eighty-five items), but my brother and I were too lazy to extend our sales pitch beyond immediate family, and so we usually topped out at a combined ten items sold, meaning our meager commission was typically no greater than $5 each, because we were incapable of sharing a "hot numbers" solar calculator (nine items) or latch hook set (ten items). Our membership in the sales club surprisingly lasted for several years, thanks mostly to the Olympic Sales Club's dedication to filling our mailbox with new catalogs and order forms, although my family's enthusiasm for purchasing chintzy wrapping paper, just so my brother and I could pocket a few bucks, quickly waned after the first year of our entrepreneurial endeavor. As a parent myself now, I can't help but think that Captain "O," the handsome, muscular mascot of the Olympic Sales Club, who resembled an off-brand Captain America, has got to be the absolute worst superhero of all time. In fact, it wouldn't be too far of a stretch to think of Captain "O" as a nefarious supervillain. Armed with attractive, full-page ads in comic books and other publications aimed at children, and with the assistance of his loyal telemarketer sidekick Peggy, Captain "O" lured ambitious kids into their very first sales scheme, with promises of "famous name prizes" or unlimited cash ($1 per item sold). So, rather than simply handing over $5 each to my brother and I, my mom, stepdad, and grandparents were coerced into paying more than ten times that amount on unwanted stationery and envelopes, and if that doesn't sound like a villainous plot, I don't know what does.

\*

It took weeks to build up the nerve to ask my mom if I could place an order from the gag gift catalog in the back of *Boys' Life Magazine*, and then it took even longer to convince her to let me order the items I wanted. Actually, there was really only one item I cared about, the x-ray specs, but I padded my order with several other inconsequential items, like itching powder and a rubber bug in a plastic ice cube. The x-ray specs were the only thing I wanted, truly needed, but I tried to downplay my hormonal desperation. The black-and-white, post-age-stamp-sized ad promised the ability to see bones through skin, but we all knew what the x-ray specs were really for. My mom knew what I wanted them for, too, and she was hesitant to order them for me, despite the undeniable fact that they were fake, but she apparently felt compelled to not endorse my desire to commit what would probably now constitute a felony. Alas, she eventually caved, and she mailed her check to the address listed on the order form clipped from the page of the magazine, but only after I gave her the cash to fully reimburse her for the cost of my purchase. My order took months to arrive, in a shabby brown envelope, and when it finally did, it seemed as though this gag gift company based out of Florida had pulled the cruelest gag of all, swapping out a horny boy's x-ray specs for an eye patch.

It only recently occurred to me that this was possibly my mom's own doing, her passive aggressive way of using irony to teach me a lesson. Either that, or I just simply wrote the wrong item number on the order form. Being in the fifth grade at the time, that's probably the case, but me being me, I've always been compelled to inject menial shit with greater meaning than it deserves.

# I Think You Loved Me More When I Used to Wear Sweatsuits

The very first time you took me home, I was wearing a sweatsuit. We had known each other for years, but this was the first time you took me home. You even said this was the first time you brought someone home who was wearing a sweatsuit, but this was no ordinary sweatsuit. This was one damn fine ENYCE sweatsuit. It was the night of your college graduation. You were in skirt and heels, and I was in sweatsuit and white Adidas. We danced to Nelly ft. Kelly Rowland—"No matter what I do, all I think about is you"—and you must have felt while we were dancing that I thought of you now as more than a friend. We had danced many times before, but this was the first time it ended with you taking me home. That night in your bedroom, I was too excited to perform—a memory that reddens my face to this day—but I put my mouth on you, and tasted you inside and out, a flavor I now know and crave. It's been years since I've worn sweatsuits. It's been years since we devoured each other like we used to, fifteen years ago, but I want you to know that I think about it constantly. Recently we were shopping in Detroit, and a damn fine sweatsuit caught my eye. "Maybe I should start wearing sweatsuits again," I said to you, and the memory of that first night together compelled me to lay my money down.

# Humiliation

Katie and I had a mutual morning off while our kids were in school, so we spent it together doing something we'd been doing more and more frequently lately, commiserating about money, and our general lack of it. The immediate topic at hand, while we drank our coffee, was the cable bill, and why it was so damn high. So, Katie began to dig, and it wasn't long before she spoke up and said, "Well, somebody ordered an adult movie for $7," and my heart skipped a beat. "Did you order a fucking porno?" Katie asked, and I reflexively lied through my teeth. "Well, if you didn't, then you better talk to the kids about what they're watching," Katie said, and the thought of what my denial implied, that I had placed the blame of ordering a pornographic movie on my own children, made me physically ill, so I quickly copped to the truth. Katie laid into me like she had rarely done before, and I felt the great weight of shame on my shoulders. "What was the title?" she asked, and I answered with a dumbfounded, "I don't know," but she didn't believe me. In all honesty, I really couldn't remember the title. I didn't even remember if it had a proper title—it wasn't even a full movie, just a fifteen-minute scene—but I remembered most other things about it, and icily relayed them, in detail, to Katie. The scene was completely vanilla. No choking or gagging or bondage. No spanking. No frills. Nothing bordering on or hinting at illegal. Just boring old heterosexual coitus, featuring Jesse Jane, one of the more surgically enhanced adult film actresses around, and some nameless hunk of meat. My description of the scene I had been charged $7 for began to make me feel exceptionally sad. "I don't believe you," Katie said, and I couldn't blame her. "Unfortunately, I'm telling the truth," I said. It appeared some of the fire had been extinguished from the argument, but our conversation was far from over. Katie asked why I felt the need to pay for something that was freely available online, and I told her that I stopped perusing internet pornography quite some time ago, out of fear of computer viruses, as well as my distaste for the increasingly hardcore, violent, and unsettling content that was overwhelmingly accessible via the web. "But couldn't you just get it for free from work?" she asked, and suddenly the conversation revealed itself to be about more than just a porno movie, or the $7 it cost.

For the past five months, I'd been working as an

assistant manager at Family Video, a midwestern chain video rental store that had an "adults only" room full of pornographic DVDs. The urge to apply for this occupation came on a whim, during a time in which I was only partially employed as an academic librarian, and after my nearly decade-long job as a university writing instructor unceremoniously came to an end. Over the years, as my dissatisfaction with academia festered, I had joked about quitting teaching and applying for a job at Family Video, but I didn't do so until my need for reliable employment reached a desperate peak. I needed a consistent full-time job, preferably with benefits, and if I didn't have to commute an hour, both ways, even better, so I applied for my first customer service job since 2003 and was hired after two interviews and a surprisingly lengthy written test. At first, it felt like a relief. I had forgotten what it felt like to simply go to work, clock in and out, and not worry about grading stacks of essays, attending faculty meetings, or replying to around-the-clock student emails. Sure, I was making a fraction of what I earned teaching three or four sections of basic composition, but the ease and mindlessness of my new job seduced me into complacency. But soon enough, that ease would turn to boredom, and as my responsibilities at Family Video grew, quickly advancing from part-time shift leader to full-time assistant manager, it became painfully clear that I simply could not afford to work there. I was all too familiar with how little teachers get paid and could truly relate to and support the fact that educators deserve a respectable wage, but at the very same time, I was living in a reality in which I had never, in my adult life, made so little money, and had so little free time, than while I was working a full-time job outside of academia, and this utter lack of money and time was a genuine source of humiliation. Granted, when I was working in higher education, I was broke, relatively speaking, but at least I was home to pick up my kids from school and help them with their homework. At least I could help around the house on the weekends. At least I was able to visit friends and family over the holidays. But while I was with Family Video, not only could I barely afford to pay the most basic of monthly bills, I was also not home to help my kids study for tests. Not only could I not afford to help my mother after she lost her job, but I couldn't even take the time off needed to help her move in with my grandmother. And when I did have a day or two off, I was too damn tired to do anything constructive. In short, I felt impotent.

So, it was a rare occasion, while my family was away on a weekend trip to Chicago, when I decided to treat myself to a little adult entertainment for the cost of $7, or about three-fourths of my pathetic hourly wage, before "commission," and when Katie discovered the extra charge on our cable bill and pointedly asked me why I couldn't have simply rented a porno from work, rather than add $7 I didn't have onto an already excessive and wholly unnecessary cable bill, I felt like she was criticizing and mocking my station in life. And perhaps rightfully so. Initially, I pathetically attempted to deceive and deflect. I tried to play the victim. I accused Katie of shaming me for having healthy sexual desires. But that wasn't the case, at all. At that moment, I felt sincere humiliation, like I'd rarely felt before. I was humiliated that I had been caught, red-handed, ordering a pornographic movie, and so I attempted to redirect the blame at Katie's feet, rather than admit that it was I who acted in error. And it wasn't simply that I had been humiliated about being caught ordering a porno, it was the humiliation of not being able to afford said pornographic movie, it was the humiliation of working in a store that rented and sold pornographic movies, it was the humiliation of failing at my previous jobs, it was the humiliation of having to start all over again, at the age of thirty-seven. It was the humiliation of realizing that all the bullshit that came before, the college degrees, the teaching appointments, the writing publications, couldn't protect me from falling flat on my ass. I wish I could say that, in my moment of humility, I apologized to Katie, not simply for charging a porno movie to our cable bill, but for failing to adequately provide for our family, but I didn't. At least, I didn't that day. But later that afternoon, I canceled our cable service, and the day after that, I began to search for another job.

# I Quit

I. Starrcade
Atlanta, Georgia
November 28, 1985


Magnum T.A. and Tully Blanchard brawl in a steel cage, but only after Magnum T.A. begins to gouge at Blanchard's lacerated forehead with a splintered chunk of wood does Blanchard scream out his resignation.

II. Clash of the Champions
Troy, New York
November 15, 1989


Ric Flair and Terry Funk chop and punch and slam and piledrive, they batter each other, yet neither man will submit, until Flair sinks in the Figure Four Leg-lock, and Funk cries, begs for release, "Yes, I quit!"

III. Royal Rumble
Anaheim, California
January 24, 1999


The Rock and Mankind do everything in their power to destroy their bodies. Nothing is off limits—tables, ladders, low blows, the ring bell—yet nothing can persuade them to forfeit the match. It requires eleven unprotected chair shots to the skull of a handcuffed Mankind before the audience hears the voice of a concussed and supine Mick Foley screech, "I quit! I quit! I quit!"

IV. Family Video
Canton, Michigan
February 21, 2017

After ten months of working minimum-wage retail management, I withdraw a cracked Samsung Galaxy S4 cellular phone from the right hip pocket of my chinos, and text the words, *fuck it i quit.*

# Participation Trophies

My son loved the uniform more than he enjoyed playing the game. He liked the accoutrements: the gloves, the helmet, the bat, the socks and stirrups, the cleats, even the jockstrap and cup. He liked to play catch and take his bat to the cages, but when it came time to step into the batter's box, he froze. He never acclimated to swinging against a pitcher who wanted to strike him out, rather than an encouraging parent or coach. Early on, he could still get on base by simply not swinging, because chances are he was going to walk or get hit by the ball if he didn't move out of the way of a wild pitch. Those first couple years after tee ball and coach pitch, he still managed to make it around the bases at least once per game, but it rapidly became less fun as coaches became more serious, parents became bigger assholes, and opposing pitchers' arms became stronger and wild pitches resulted in tears and bruises, rather than an easy walk to first base. Still, he lasted four years. He advanced from tee ball to coach pitch to Livonia YMCA co-ed baseball. He played for the Mudcats, the Twins, and the Rangers. He never had to try out, he never got cut from a team, as long as his mom and I paid the cost to play, and yes, at the end of each season, his entire team received the maligned participation trophy, no matter their record of wins over losses. But my son played, goddamn it, which is more than I can say for myself. As much as I loved baseball, and obsessed over baseball cards and all things Jose Canseco, I never once put on a baseball jersey that wasn't emblazoned with another player's name. One summer, between the fourth and fifth grades, I tried out for the local traveling team, the Onalaska Royals, and I didn't make the cut. I was invited to the "c team," and I quit, on the spot. Then again, about five years later, during the spring of my freshman year, I tried out for my high school baseball team, and was promptly removed from the equation, and driven to the emergency room by my grandfather, when the tip of my left middle finger was crushed while attempting to bunt. And that was the end of my illustrious baseball career. Never once did I step behind the plate during an officiated game of baseball, but my son earned four years of game-worn jerseys and hats. His face is on four years of team portraits and baseball cards, which are proudly displayed on my desk in clear, plastic top-loaders. And his participation trophies are some of the only trophies I own. My son stopped playing baseball when the game stopped being fun. But me? Shit, I didn't even participate.

# In Silence

Try as I might, I find it near impossible to sit in silence, though I find this to be a most admirable trait. Sitting in silence, without a single distraction. It may be odd, but this is what I remember most about my grandfather. Sitting in silence, in the kitchen, in the cabin, in the forest, with nothing but a cigarette and a cup of black coffee. Sometimes with the radio turned on, but with the volume turned down to a near inaudible level, just enough to barely register that someone, somewhere is saying something. Talk radio. Never music. Never music. Just voices. Faint voices. Apparitions. In the dark. Hours before sunrise. Even on Saturday and Sunday mornings. Especially then. Sitting in the dark, in silence, with a cigarette and a cup of black coffee. This, to me, is the mark of a man. My grandfather. Sitting in silence, in the dark, with a cigarette and a cup of black coffee. Comfortable in his thoughts. Comfortable in the silence. Me? I need as many distractions as I can get. Headphones on, bass-heavy music assaulting my ears. A laptop computer or book in my hands. Uncooked Pop-Tart in my mouth. And lots of creamy white milk in my coffee. This, among many other things, makes me less than. Less than a man.

A lesser man. Uncomfortable with the thoughts in my own head. Unbearable thoughts. Nauseating thoughts. I tell myself, "I'm bored," but over and over again, I keep hearing the words, "There's no such thing as boredom, only fear," and these words are correct. I fear. I am afraid. Which also makes me a lesser man. Unlike my grandfather. I tried it this morning. Sitting in silence, in the dark, before dawn, with a scalding hot cup of black coffee, Folgers Instant, minus the cream (I skipped the cigarette, altogether), and barely made it three minutes. "I'm fucking bored," I said to myself, and immediately heard the requisite response, "There is no boredom, only fear," but I've got no patience for either, today.

# Raccoons Ain't Nothing to Fuck With

Not long after my mother got a divorce, she began to bribe me to come visit her new apartment by offering to let me stay out as late as I wanted. I was seventeen years old, at the time, and living with my grandparents, while my brother stayed with his dad, and my mom lived in public housing with my two young sisters. I could waltz through the door after 3 a.m., red-eyed and sour-breathed, no questions asked, as long as I slept in my mother's apartment. I would go out with my friends, who all had similarly liberal curfews, and get blackout drunk and stoned, and then stumble up to my mom's door, while a family of well-fed raccoons raided her garbage cans. I came to see those raccoons quite a lot, the fat mother raccoon reared up on her hind legs, fearlessly hissing if I came too close to her litter, who gorged themselves on decomposing refuse. From a relatively young age, I was taught that raccoons "ain't nothing to fuck with." Back when I used to go hunting with my grandfather, he warned me that if I ever saw a raccoon coming toward me in the wild, shoot it. Put it down, without a second thought. Raccoons were vicious and filthy animals, I was told. They carried rabies. And the only thing worse than a raccoon was a feral cat. So, imagine my surprise when, one evening, nearly a decade after my nights of getting sloshed and passing out on my mother's living room couch, I was sitting in my car, in a McDonald's parking lot, waiting to meet my grandparents, who were driving across three states to visit my new home in Michigan, and I saw a feral cat leading a family of raccoons into a McDonald's dumpster. At first, the raccoons stayed in the rear, under cover of the tall, marsh grass, then the feral cat came out to conduct reconnaissance. She made sure the coast was clear, and then came the mother raccoon, big as a healthy, midsized dog, followed by five or six cubs. The raccoons climbed up into the gated dumpster, where they feasted on leftover Big Macs and Chicken McNuggets, while the feral cat kept watch. My grandparents were running late, so I just sat there, in the McDonald's parking lot, until the feral cat and raccoons finished their meal and then retreated into the marsh, their bellies full of greasy fast food. When my grandparents' van finally pulled into the McDonald's, I had a new anecdote to share with them, and even though my mistrust of raccoons and feral cats wasn't assuaged by this one encounter, I could, at least, empathize with them, being that I too often filled my body with trash.

# Proverbs 19:17

*He that hath pity upon the poor lendeth unto the LORD;*
*and that which he hath given will he pay him again.*

A wiry, tattooed man who closely resembled a card-carrying member of the Aryan Nation stood in the rear entrance of the laundromat, holding the door ajar while smoking a menthol cigarette and conversing with the absurdly tall woman who managed the place. When they finished their muted, but genial, conversation, the man flipped his cigarette far away into a puddle, properly closed the double-hinged glass door, and turned his attention to the nearby vintage arcade game. The tattooed man began feeding the game quarter after quarter, $4 or $5 worth, at least. Galaga only required one quarter per credit, but clearly the man had staked his claim for the remainder of the morning. He played with passion and intensity, the clatter of his playing louder than the tinny, robotic music and effects, but he was respectful of the game. He played hard, but he was not abusive. He groaned and yelped and gritted his teeth and worked the muscles in his jaw when he failed, when he lost another quarter, but not a single curse escaped his mouth. He was dressed unremarkably—steel-toe work boots, Levi's, and a wrinkled t-shirt—but he was wearing black leather driving gloves, as though he was behind the wheel of an Aston Martin, rather than manipulating the battered joystick of a thirty-year-old video game. It was a Sunday morning, 10 a.m., give or take a minute or two, and the laundromat was running on full capacity. The sudsy chug of washers and the whining spin of high-speed dryers. The radio in the corner alternated between Evangelical sermon and syrupy Contemporary Christian soft rock. A group of elderly men and women nonsensically chattered about German chocolate cake. A trio of hungover frat boys in smelly-looking, dingy sweatpants folded stained sheets while eating miniature bags of Cool Ranch Doritos. Above it all, the scent of fabric softener and bleach. The tattooed man played on, chasing his personal high score, and when he'd finally run through every last one of his quarters, he removed his gloves, drew a long, hard pull from a plastic bottle of tepid Mtn Dew, and fixed his rheumy eyes on the game screen. It was once common practice for arcade games to regurgitate mundane slogans like "Say No to Drugs" and "Stay in School," but somebody had programmed the laundromat's version of Galaga so that, in between plays, the screen flashed the words "Proverbs 19:17." This was the mantra of the laundromat. It was written on the walls. It was stenciled on the vinyl laundry bags that the laundromat sold for six bucks apiece. But the tattooed man didn't care, or more aptly didn't give a shit, what these words and numbers meant or represented or signified. All he cared about was the game. Other men and women came to the laundromat with plastic baskets full of soiled socks and underwear and dish towels, but the tattooed man had come, and would leave, empty-handed. Considering how much change he'd spent, he would actually leave the laundromat with less than he came. Surely, he felt lighter. His hip pocket far less full. And yet, while he felt an immeasurable sense of pride when he saw nearly the entire leaderboard, top to bottom, filled with his three initials—his signature— the few remaining spaces that belonged to other players provoked him to play on.

# Be Dialing!

Don West, poet laureate of home shopping networks, bullhorn-voiced, mustachioed pitchman supreme, is selling a Michael Jordan card, and not just any Michael Jordan card, but a refractor, an oversized, limited edition, serialized, Upper Deck, authenticated, Command Performer refractor, the most resplendent of all Michael Jordan refractors, and when you order this Michael Jordan refractor, you also get a Shawn Kemp refractor, and a Penny Hardaway refractor, as well as a selection of not one, not two, not three, but four, count 'em four, National Hero commemorative die-cuts, but only while supplies last, so "Be dialing, folks!" because there's only thirty-one sets remaining.

Don West insists that the Michael Jordan refractor, alone, is trading for up to $200—"If you're lucky enough to find him!"—but despite this, he's selling the Michael Jordan refractor, along with the Kemp and Hardaway refractors, as well as the Gretsky, Ripken, Griffey, and Marino National Hero die-cuts, for $149.95 total. "That's $21 and some change per card!" Don West's similarly coiffed lackey interjects, solar calculator in hand.

"*HOW* can they do that?"

I know the scam. I'm familiar with Don West's home shopping sideshow circus, but I don't care, I'm all in. I pick up my phone and proceed to dial, just like Don West tells me to do. The Michael Jordan refractor is from 1996, so this *Shop At Home* segment originally aired over 20 years ago, and still, I dial the number on the screen, aware that the "National Hero Commemorative Refractor Blowout" is sold out, and the phone number is long since out of service. "Be dialing!" Don West implores, and I dutifully comply.

# Poke

My daughter was given an assignment to research our family and present to her class what made us unique, but I've always been of the mind that what truly made my family unique was how little we knew about our family. My daughter's biological mother was adopted, I never knew my father, and my maternal grandfather never knew his dad, either.

Our family tree was marred by missing limbs.

And so, we started to dig on *Ancestry.com*, and what we found brought tears to my eyes. There on the screen was my maternal great-grandmother's Petition for Naturalization. I saw, for the very first time, her full birth name, her birthplace, the name of the ship she and her parents sailed over from Italy, as well as the date they arrived on the eastern shore. There, at the bottom of the page, was her looping, calligraphic signature, a true contrast to her husband's, scribbled on his World War II draft registration card, his first as a U.S. citizen, in the year 1942, at the age of fifty-nine.

He had the handwriting of a child.

And then, the very next day, while researching my grandfather's side of the family, I found the name of his biological father, and not just his mother's second husband, whom everybody referred to as his dad—not unlike my own situation, something I was not infrequently reminded of, back when I found myself deep in trouble, over my head, in the weeds, as I often was, crying on my grandparents' couch, needing to be bailed out, because of bounced checks, failing grades, criminal charges, my first child gestating in her mother's womb.

(This one she was going to keep.)

I liked to use the excuse that I never knew my father. It was easy to drum up, and I would spring quick, fresh tears, and my grandfather would attempt to console me, provide comfort by reminding me that he never knew his father either, that he too was a bastard, but he hoped that I might someday accept him as a father.

Like how he accepted me as his son.

He didn't know his dad because his dad was in prison. That's what I discovered that he never revealed to me. And when I first learned of that, five years after my grandfather's death, I wondered if he ever actually knew that's why his father wasn't at home. And so, I asked my mom, but she simply replied by suggesting that I look up my own dad, as well.

He wasn't difficult to find.

He's on Facebook, just like everybody else's dad, just like me, a father of two myself. He sells timeshares and posts motivational, quasi-spiritual memes. I've thought about creating a fake account and friending him or sending him a private message. Or maybe I'll just poke him once and then never contact him ever again and hope that the irony sticks.

# PWI

I used to take regular trips alone with my grandparents. We would usually drive, the three of us together in my grandfather's car, to visit my grandfather's family in Waukesha, Wisconsin, or my grandmother's family in Chicago, but my grandmother and I would occasionally travel by ourselves, just the two of us, and since she never learned to drive we would take the Amtrak from LaCrosse, Wisconsin, to Union Station, in Chicago. At the time, the five-or-six-hour train ride felt excruciatingly long, an eternity, and being without the luxury of a Walkman or Gameboy, most of my time was spent staring out the window, coping with motion sickness, while my grandmother smoked Benson & Hedges cigarettes, and occasionally dropped ashes on my thigh. But on one such occasion, when I was about the age of ten, around the year 1989, my grandmother must have taken notice of just how bored I was, and she purchased something from a newsstand to keep me occupied. It was an issue of *Pro Wrestling Illustrated*, a magazine dedicated to exploring the subject of, you guessed it, professional wrestling. Now, the purchase of such a magazine, in and of itself, wasn't necessarily an odd choice. I was then, like many if not most children at the time, a fan of professional wrestling. I was, in essence, a Hulkamaniac, saying my prayers and taking my vitamins. But unlike the more readily known *WWF Magazine*, which I was a frequent reader of, *Pro Wrestling Illustrated* did not exclusively focus on the goings-on of Vincent Kennedy McMahon's World Wrestling Federation. *Pro Wrestling Illustrated* was not a promotional product owned and published by the WWF, and so it did not feature glossy color pictorials celebrating the greatness of Hulk Hogan and the Ultimate Warrior. In addition to Jake "The Snake" Roberts and Shawn Michaels, *Pro Wrestling Illustrated* seemed just as invested in discussing "The Nature Boy" Ric Flair and Kerry Von Erich and "The American Dream" Dusty Rhodes, long before they made their big leap to WWF. There was frequent mention of WWF's regional and global competition, such as WCW, NWA, AWA, NJPW, and AAA. There were gritty, black-and-white photographs of bloodied and battered men, such as Terry Funk, Cactus Jack, and Abdullah the Butcher, in the midst of brutal "hardcore" barbed-wire matches. The pages of *Pro Wrestling Illustrated* were of newsprint quality, and the magazine, as a whole, portrayed an almost obscene tone, in my ten-year-old mind. I cannot lie, at the time, I preferred *WWF Magazine*. *Pro Wrestling Illustrated* made me uncomfortable, even slightly nauseated, like the first time I saw a pornographic movie, in the seventh grade (*Gazongas 2*). There was a gritty honesty to *Pro Wrestling Illustrated* that I just was not prepared for. If *WWF Magazine* was analogous to the *Sports Illustrated Swimsuit Issue*, air-brushed and commercial and virginal, *Pro Wrestling Illustrated* was the waterlogged issue of *Hustler* discovered under a conspicuously placed rock, hidden in the woods, and at the age of ten, riding the Amtrak with my grandmother, I wasn't quite ready for *Hustler*.

## Attack at the Yack 2

ECW chants erupted from a small gathering of fans outside the Benjamin F. Yack Arena, in Wyandotte, Michigan. Sabu and Shane Douglas were both scheduled to appear in XICW's Attack at the Yack 2, so I got my hopes up, thinking that one or both of those former ECW (Extreme Championship Wrestling) champions were making an early parking lot cameo, but it was just because a fan was wearing an ECW t-shirt.

While waiting for the first match to begin, but after the comic con/fanfest portion of the day concluded, I found a seat in the general admission bleachers that overlooked the center of the ring, and while the bleachers never completely filled up, it wasn't long before I was flanked on both sides by other eager fans. To my right was a married couple who were regular XICW (Xtreme Intense Championship Wrestling) attendees. The wife was a diehard fan, a true believer, who knew the first names of the ring crew and waved hello to other regulars in attendance, but was completely oblivious to any other pro wrestling, whatsoever. I found it admirable that this woman was so utterly devoted to her local pro wrestling organization but couldn't care less about the WWE (World Wrestling Entertainment). Her husband, however, was at least somewhat familiar with other pro wrestling promotions, based upon his references to Jinder Mahal and Jack Swagger, but he said he pretty much exclusively just followed XICW now, or at least he did so for his wife, who was the real fan of the pair.

To my left, and on the opposite end of the pro wrestling fandom spectrum, was a belt guy. You know, one of those guys who walks around wrestling events with a replica belt over his shoulder. If I had come with a friend, or my son, as I usually did, I probably would've just talked to whoever I'd come with, and completely ignored the belt guy, but I was there alone, and belt guy was there alone, and so it wasn't long before we began to talk . . . about his belt, of course. I'll admit it, I don't know much about pro wrestling belts, it's just not something I've ever paid much attention to, but it was entertaining, listening to this guy lovingly dote over his belt and talk shit about the other belt guys and gals who walked by. As of that day, he'd amassed a modest, but no less impressive, collection of A-list signatures upon his belt: Edge, Chris

Jericho, Batista, Big Show, Daniel Bryan. Most of the autographs he acquired while attending AutoRama, "America's Premiere Custom Car Series," which made an annual stop in Detroit and always had at least one WWE superstar in attendance. But thanks to Attack at the Yack 2, belt guy had a few new signatures on his "big gold belt": Ron Simmons, Sabu, and Shane Douglas.

There was no doubt about it, I had come way earlier than I needed, but I wasn't sure how much time I'd need to make my way around the comic con/fanfest portion of the event. As it turns out, I had about three extra hours between when I finished up with the comic con, and when the first match of the night began, and so I burned some daylight walking around downtown Wyandotte, eating a sandwich in a Jimmy John's that was pouring water from the ceiling, downing a few cheap lukewarm beers from the concession stand, making conversation with my fellow wrestling fans, people-watching, and taking occasional notes. Being that the event was promoted as a comic con/fanfest during the day, and then a wrestling show at night, there were a select few individuals who were clearly more interested in the comic con portion of the day, and so there were two

Jedis in attendance, lightsabers in hand, walking around among the attendees in wrestling shirts. There was a vendor who was dressed as a convincing Undertaker, minus the prescription eyeglasses, as well some dude who wore a generic luchador mask and cape. But for the most part, the folks in Yack Arena were dressed in casual street clothes, with a significant percentage in basketball shorts and assorted wrestling t-shirts. I've always been hesitant to wear wrestling shirts to wrestling events, not unlike how I never wear band shirts to concerts. I just can't handle the pressure and judgement. But this day was an exception. I was wearing my New Japan Pro Wrestling "Lion Mark" baseball tee, simply because it was the best-fitting t-shirt I owned. As far as I saw, I was one of two people wearing an NJPW shirt, with the other being a colorful Jushin Thunder Liger t-shirt. And of course, there was no shortage of the ubiquitous Bullet Club tee, which is now sold at all Hot Topic locations, when they're not sold out, but there was an ample amount of Insane Clown Posse and juggalo-affiliated shirts and memorabilia to help balance it all out.

Shortly before the first match, a last minute "dark match" addition, crowd activity began to pick up, and I noticed a familiar face mingling with the fans. It was a larger-than-average white man with a trim goatee and shaved head. He was wearing a sleeveless denim shirt, and light-wash dad jeans. He made his way through the crowd, shaking hands and posing for pictures while he sipped a beer, until he stopped right in front of me. We made eye contact, and I suddenly recognized him as "The Franchise" Shane Douglas. I played it cool and gave him a nod of recognition and raised my beer to him, and he did so back in return. Throughout the night, I saw Shane holding court with fans and talent alike, and he looked to be having a good old time. During the first match, while Journey's "Don't Stop Believing," and then "Wheels in the Sky," played over the venue's PA system, Shane could be seen in the corner of the fanfest area, play-fighting with Sabu, and later, as his match drew closer, Shane grew rowdier, and playfully tossed around empty folding chairs, like he would have done back in his ECW glory days.

Overall, the card was entertaining, start to finish, with standout moments including what could be referred to as a "cupcake spot," in which "The Genetic Jackpot" Joe Coleman received a cupcake to the face while XICW

Lightweight Champion Johnny Devine held him in a post-match camel clutch, and I was thoroughly delighted to watch as ring veteran The DBA, or The Detroit Bad Ass, also known as the owner/promoter of XICW, soaked his elbow pad in lighter fluid, set it on fire, and then dropped a top rope flaming elbow onto his recumbent opponent. And I might not be a regular XICW attendee, to the extent of the married couple I made conversation with throughout the length of the evening, but I had previously come on more than one occasion, and was happy to see area favorites like "Sweet" Willy Watts, who I briefly met during intermission and congratulated after his successful tag team match, and Jake Something, who held the tag team titles with Hakim Zane (known collectively as "The Purge"), but lost a six-man, loser leaves XICW match to the formerly mentioned DBA, MM3 (DBA's son), and Jaimy Coxxx. Over the years, I'd seen Jake Something wrestle on several Metro Detroit cards, including a dark match for Ring of Honor, and based upon the loser leaves XICW stipulation, I assumed that Jake and his tag team partner Hakim Zane were on to greener pastures, but maybe they'd come back next week under masks, I joked to my new friends. There was also a good old fashioned no-disqualification match featuring the "homicidal, suicidal, genocidal" Sabu, and former WWE fan favorite D-Lo Brown. Sabu and D-Lo's match was completely void of any sort of technical skill, but it was one hell of a barn burner, considering the age of the combatants, and featured a barrage of chair shots, including a match-ending chair-aided diving leg drop from Sabu, which D-Lo sold in an Oscar-caliber performance that had me thinking that he honestly might have been concussed.

And then there was the main event, featuring Mahabali Shera, who was taking a short break from Impact/Global Force Wrestling, and the returning XICW Xtreme Intense Champion, Shane Douglas. Shera was greeted with a smattering of unenthusiastic and casually racist Jinder Mahal chants, which thankfully didn't catch on, but the crowd was pumped for Shane Douglas. *But wait a second*, I thought to myself, *that's not Shane Douglas!* Shane Douglas was still hovering around behind the curtain somewhere. I didn't know who this blond, clean-shaven man with the XICW Xtreme Intense belt thought he was. And then I came to the realization that the man I'd mistaken for Shane Douglas wasn't actually Shane Douglas, and I felt like a complete idiot. All night long, I'd been amused by how cordial and playful Shane Douglas had been with his fans and fellow wrestlers, but as it turns out, that wasn't Shane Douglas, at all. The man who I misidentified as Shane Douglas did eventually become involved in the match, and was introduced as Rough House Rob, but after I came to terms with my mistake, I pretty much lost interest in the match, and I was simply counting down the minutes until I could make my exit and begin my drive home.

After the bell rang, and Shane Douglas successfully retained his XICW Xtreme Intense Championship, with the help of "not Shane Douglas," I didn't stick around for any post-match announcements or shenanigans. It had been a long day, a solid eight hours, at least, and I was more than ready to go home. Belt Guy disappeared long before the main event, but I said goodbye to the married couple that befriended and educated me on all things XICW. I promised them I'd attend a regular, weekly show, and not just these bigger, special events, and told them that if I didn't see them before then, I'd look out for them in October, when XICW made its return to historic Cobo Hall. Insane Clown Posse was scheduled to appear, along with Jim Cornette and Bobby "The Brain" Heenan (RIP). I wouldn't miss it for the world.

The night after XICW's show in Cobo Hall, I heard ru-
mors of WWE's debut appearance in Detroit's brand-
spanking-new Little Caesar's Arena, and I'll admit that
when I first saw the official advertisement and learned
that the event in question would be none other than Hell
in a Cell, a first for the city of Detroit, I couldn't wait to
order my tickets. But the more that I thought about it,
the more my excitement waned. Not unlike a growing
number of pro wrestling fans, I think much more now
about where my money goes when I buy tickets for a
wrestling event, and as much as I thought I'd like to attend WWE's Little Caesar's Arena debut, I have diffi-
culty rationalizing dropping that kind of money into the
McMahon family trust, when instead it could go directly
to local talent, and the XICW. I imagine that a number
of Metro Detroit pro wrestling fans will have to make
the difficult decision of choosing one event over the other, either XICW or WWE, and that more than a few
will choose the big-league spectacle and pyrotechnics of
WWE. But the WWE doesn't need my help generat-
ing revenue, and so if I must pick one over the other, I'd
rather support the legacy of Detroit professional wrestling, and do what little I can to help the XICW drop a
flaming elbow on their competition.

# Bed Bugs

I was headed towards a garbage can, to throw away an empty cup of coffee, and suddenly caught a strong whiff of mint. Before I even saw the young man brushing his teeth over the garbage can, I had smelled his toothpaste, and there he was, in faded blue jeans and a hooded sweatshirt, a full backpack slung over his shoulder. "What are you doing, you fucking bum?" an assertive male voice inquired from a distance, and the young man brushing his teeth took a swig from his water bottle, spit a mouthful of foam into the garbage can, and laughed so hard he nearly choked. "What the fuck does it look like?" the young man replied. "You're gonna be late for class, dude!" the distant voice chimed in, and the young man who had been brushing his teeth jogged away from the garbage can to catch up with his classmate and disappeared in the crowd.

With the garbage can no longer occupied, I dropped my empty cup into the foamy puddle of spit that had already begun to attract bees. Several of them lazily flew up out of the can, and when I felt something crawling on the lobe of my right ear, I tried, at first, not to panic, but being deathly allergic to bees, couldn't stop myself from swatting wildly at my head. Luckily, it was only a ladybug. "Another fucking ladybug!" I said out loud, to myself. They were coming off me like spores. Already that day, I had found at least five of them on me. Or maybe it was the same one, returning after I brushed it off the sleeve of my moth-eaten sweater.

Later that afternoon, while walking with Katie, one of those rare moments when we were able to synchronize our schedules and grab lunch together, I mentioned that ladybugs were flying out of my orifices and was deftly corrected. She said that they were more than likely Japanese Stink Beetles, which didn't sound nearly as magical, but did, in my opinion, seem more appropriate. "And speaking of bugs . . . ." I grumbled while nudging Katie's elbow and nodding my head in the direction of a large, white truck being loaded up by men in coveralls and rubber gloves. Two by two, they paraded from a student apartment complex a series of twin-size mattresses wrapped in plastic. "Bed bugs," Katie gasped. "Ugh, that's gonna give me nightmares," I said, and it did.

# What She Expects Me to Do

Don—a fifty-four-year-old schizophrenic—is 5'2", bald, white, round as a bowling ball, and he's stalking my mom. Don and my mom are neighbors. They live in the same apartment building, low-income housing for the elderly and disabled, even though my fifty-seven-year-old mother is technically neither, although close to both. Don has been sliding hand-written notes underneath my mother's door. *You're disgusting*, one note said. *You're disgusting, leave now*, said another. "Don likes you," my mom's floormates tell her. "You remind him of his dead girlfriend," they say, and imply she's been leading him on, because she had the audacity to treat him like a human being. One night, Don stole my mother's laundry—two loads of wet towels, bathmats, and her treasured denim Dickies overalls—then returned it, dried and folded, piece by piece. Don vandalized her car, too—a minivan she inherited from my grandfather. Bit by bit, Don cuts away at the front grill of my mom's minivan. When my mom tells all of this to my grandmother, my grandmother laughs and laughs, and when my mom relays this information to me, she's half-laughing herself, but I tell her I don't think it's the slightest bit funny. She reassures me she's not afraid of Don, then confesses she sleeps with a wooden chair wedged against the door, and keeps a hammer, a screwdriver, and a serrated kitchen knife underneath her bed, just in case. "I'm not going to tell you Don's full name," she says without my asking. "I don't want you to look him up and kick his ass." But then she does exactly that because that's what she expects me to do.

# Piece by Piece

Katie told me not to do it, but how could I not? "It's money," I said, my response to just about everything lately. The procedure itself might not have been too risky, but Katie was worried about the possibility of infection. "$250 for ten hours," was my justification, "$25 an hour," and my mind was made up. At an hourly rate like that, I thought, I'd be willing to do this full-time, forty hours a week. I'd be set, then. No more job applications, no more interviews, just revenue. And I'd barely have to lift a finger. Hell, I'd be contributing to a good cause, saving lives even, I told myself.

The description of the procedure I received from the research team was appropriately clinical. They informed me that I'd begin the day by receiving a double IV, one with insulin and one with sugar. Throughout the day, my blood sugar would be carefully monitored, and while this was taking place, a doctor would make a small incision in my leg, about a quarter of an inch long, and take three muscle biopsies. They said the amount of flesh removed would be about the size of a pea, but it was unclear if that estimate referred to the combined size of the three samples, or if it was one pea per biopsy. Either way, I said yes, I'd do it.

Most of the folks to whom I mentioned this new money-making opportunity didn't seem to understand why I would volunteer to be sliced open. "Are you sick?" they asked with genuine concern. Was this something I had to do for my own health? But I told them it was just about the money (and maybe just a little bit for the story). "Sounds like it'll hurt," they'd say next, and I assured them that I'd receive a local anesthetic, Lidocaine, "the same anesthetic that dentists use in their procedures," but truth be told, I wanted it to hurt.

For the past three years, my employment situation had been unstable, to say the least, and for the past year, it had become downright dire, but not for a lack of effort. According to my own personal records, I had applied to well over sixty jobs in a little over one year, and for my troubles, I had received a grand total of nine interviews and a ten-month stint as a minimum-wage video store assistant manager. But for the last six weeks, after quitting my job at the video store, I'd been unemployed. I was thirty-eight years old, with three college degrees, two of them master's, and I was contributing absolutely nothing, while Katie tirelessly worked her fingers to the bone.

And that is why I wanted the procedure to hurt. I felt like I deserved to be in agony, physical pain, and not just the mental and emotional discomfort I was experiencing. The money was almost an afterthought. In the scheme of things, $250 might not pay for much more than a week of groceries, as essential as that is for a family of four (plus a dog), but the pain, I hoped, and the scar, would last. If I could slice off little pea-sized morsels of myself, and give them directly to Katie, I would, but in the end, I didn't have to. In the end, Katie talked me out of the procedure, like no other person could. Like no other person would. But just in case she ever changes her mind, my blade is ready, and she can cut off as much of me as she wants, piece by pea-sized piece.

# Black River

I remember the pull of the Black River, the current washing me downstream, attempting to tread water, the soaked weight of my clothes, the water up around my neck, the wake in my ears, the riverbank too far in the distance, the rank smell and taste of the Black River, cold even in July. Sometimes I think I didn't make it to shore. Maybe I was just another boy taken by the Black River. What would my friends have done? What could they do? How long would it take to call for help, to call the police, to call an ambulance? Surely, I would have been long dead, body cold, sunk to the muddy floor of the Black River, like the other boys, dead in the river. People pretend they don't understand. They create conspiracies. It had to be a man who drowned all of those boys. They pretend they don't understand the pull of the Black River. By the time I decided to jump in, several of my friends had already swam to the other side. It looked so close, a stone's throw away, and I made it across, oh so slowly, but I did it, I made it to the other side, where my friends made fun of me for swimming with my shirt on. But I underestimated how much the Black River had taken out of me. My heart pounded, and my lungs burned. If I was thinking clearly, if I wasn't thirteen or fourteen years old, maybe I would've taken the long way back, maybe I would've walked the bridge over the Black River, past Hardee's, but I wasn't thinking clearly, and I was thirteen or fourteen years old, and I didn't want to walk the bridge over the Black River and risk being seen in the wet clothes stuck to my soft, androgynous body. And so, I jumped back into the Black River, and was immediately winded, the pull of the current so much stronger, the water so much colder, no longer refreshing, no longer rejuvenating, just ice cold, cold to the bone. My mouth filled with water as I sucked air. My belly filled with the Black River. My friends were no longer visible at the shore. I had floated so far downriver the houseboats were now unrecognizable. We jumped off the dock of a neighbor's houseboat, but now I was near the end of the park, where the Black River opened into the Mississippi, and I knew that I was dead. Sometimes I think maybe I did die, maybe everything that followed was an afterlife hallucination, surviving the Black River, making it to shore, my friends mocking me as a I stumbled up the street, exhausted, spent, my wet jean shorts and t-shirt sticking to my soft body, being called "Free Willy" as I pretended to laugh and not think about drowning. I often think about the pull of the Black River, and how, on that day, I would've rather drowned, I would've rather been another boy at the bottom of the Black River, than let my friends see me with my shirt off.

# On the Fifth Anniversary of Taking My Daughter to Warped Tour 2013

*"Sell out . . . with me, oh yeah" —Reel Big Fish, "Sell Out"*

I was informed at the gate that I wouldn't need a ticket to enter, because I was accompanying my fourteen-year-old daughter, and several of her underage friends, so I tried to sell my extra ticket at the door and was almost immediately arrested for scalping.

Thankfully, I was not apprehended, which allowed me the opportunity to witness a Stefan Struve doppelganger get knocked out cold in a parking-lot mosh pit fist-fight, while Reel Big Fish covered A-ha's "Take On Me."

# Low Years

There's years of my life I don't talk about. There's years of my life I won't write about. There's years of my life I refuse to romanticize with poetry.

There's years of my life that if I told you what I did, or how I behaved, or how I treated the ones I loved, I'd become an instant pariah.

I thank god I came of age before social media and digital fingerprints. I thank god I grew up without a high-definition camera in my pocket. I thank god I didn't join Facebook until I turned thirty-three.

I thank god the only remnants of those low years are fading memories, an uncashed inmate release check, and an eighteen-year-old daughter who documents her father's mistakes on twitter.

# Musk

I spent my last day of unemployment doing what I could to pull my own weight—errands, household chores, preparing dinner. I burned up a few afternoon hours making *stracotto*, also known as Italian pot roast, and helped myself to a couple glasses of the dry red wine used for braising. I'm a "big guy"—I can drive after two glasses of wine—and so I still picked up my daughter from work, but on the way back, less than a few blocks away from home, I stopped the car for an injured skunk in the middle of the road.

It was early evening, but there was still plenty of sunlight, so I thought to myself, there's no way that can be a live skunk, as though it might be an animatronic toy or a black cat with a white painted stripe, like in a Pepé Le Pew cartoon, but sure enough it was. A woman by the side of the road tried to wave me by. "Go around!" she said, clearly annoyed that I'd stopped, but I was afraid of getting sprayed, even if I was in a moving vehicle. I didn't want to accidentally run it over, either, but then I thought maybe that's the best thing I could do. I should put the suffering thing out of its misery, rather than sit there and watch, along with an ever-growing audience of cellphone voyeurs, while the skunk coiled and writhed in the street. Someone laid on their horn, and I noticed the line of automobiles that had accumulated behind me. "Why did you stop?" my daughter asked in a Xanax haze, seemingly unaware of the animal in front of us. "There's a goddamn skunk in the middle of the road," I said. "I think it's hurt." My daughter was still recovering from various injuries of the past year, as well, wounds that were her story to tell, when she was ready to tell them. She was eighteen years old now, an adult, while I barely felt like one, myself. More and more frequently, when we're in public together, we get weird looks and the occasional question. "And your relationship is . . .?" My mother and I used to get these looks and questions, too, being less than eighteen years apart, but while my mother beamed at the thought that she and I were mistaken for siblings or, you know, something else, I'm disturbed by the implication that my daughter and I may be something "more." "Can't you just go around?" Gabriella asked while concentrating on her phone, but instead I decided to maneuver a Y-turn, and a passenger in the vehicle directly to my rear shot me the bird.

For the rest of the night, I couldn't shake the sadness I felt for that wounded skunk. I hoped that before it died, or before somebody ended its pain, that it had the opportunity to express its glands one final time, and when I drove down that same street the very next morning, on my way to work for the first time in eight weeks, it was devoid of traffic, human and animal alike, but there lingered a faint whiff of musk.

.

# To the Man on Karmada Street Frying Eggs in His Underwear

I can see you, you know? I can see you. I'm not trying to see you, but you're difficult to ignore. Your window is open, and your lights are on. And you're standing in front of your stove—fork in one hand, skillet in the other—wearing no more than a white undershirt and black bikini-brief underwear. I can see you from the sidewalk, where my dog has stopped to shit. I can't imagine I'm the first to see you tonight, but maybe I'm lucky. Maybe it was meant to be. Maybe our paths were destined to cross. But unless I go up and knock on your window or ring your doorbell, chances are you'll remain oblivious. And of course, I'm going to stay right here on the sidewalk, and when my dog has finished squatting, I'm going to bag his droppings and continue on with my walk. You're going to remain completely unaware of my presence, but I am going to remember you for a long time. You have given me a gift. You have enlivened my otherwise forgettable night. And, for that, I must thank you. You look so natural, so comfortable. More comfortable than I have ever felt in my own skin. I assume that even if you knew that I could see you, you would not care, and maybe even that's what you desire. Maybe you've been standing there, in front of your stove, in clear view of the entire neighborhood, all night long. Maybe you've been waiting for someone to come knock on your window or ring your doorbell. Maybe you're making enough eggs for two.

# Who Let the Dogs Out?

Instead of buying a new costume for Kelso, our seven-year-old Aussie/Collie mix, we repurposed an easy one from years before, and strapped a small rubber jockey to his harness. All of the puppy parents at the doggy daycare Halloween party kept referring to Kelso as a jockey, although technically he was the horse in the horse and jockey relationship, but still I failed to correct them, not wanting to be the asshole who insists the green guy with the bolts in his neck is actually "Frankenstein's Monster," not Frankenstein. There were no fewer than three dogs dressed like Wonder Woman, and one as Robin (Batman's young ward). Diego the Chihuahua was a piñata, Nigel the Corgi was a sushi roll, and Gladys the Leonberger, who was only eight months old and already nearing a hundred pounds, required no costume. The party was professionally catered. We ate sliders, potato salad, hand-cut potato chips, and Chicago-style hot dogs, and I discreetly shared my scraps with Kelso. There was not one but two live DJs, both of them dressed in flashy evening clubwear—one with a silver fedora—and they switched tracks as each dog was called to the stage. For Manny the Miniature Poodle, who was dressed like

Beetlejuice and accompanied by his mother, who was either dressed like Winona Ryder or just an aging goth, the DJ played "Jump in the Line" by Harry Belafonte. For Goose the Australian Shepherd, who was dressed like a werewolf, they played "Werewolves of London." And when the DJ couldn't find a suitable track to match the dog/costume combination, they played "Who Let the Dogs Out," the innocuous Baja Men hit. The costume contest was judged by three local "celebrities," one of which was the owner of a bakery (for humans), who wore a full Scooby-Doo costume. Most of the contest entrants won a prize, and even those who didn't, such as Kelso, received a complimentary bag of treats. From start to finish, the entire event was little more than two hours long, and being the grand soiree that it was, almost no one shat on the floor.

# To BUNT, or not to BUNT

On July 28, 2019, I downloaded Topps BUNT, a digital baseball card trading app. This was far from the first time I downloaded this particular app, but I had previously sworn to myself that this was something I'd never do again. I couldn't remember exactly how long it had been since I last opened BUNT on my phone but based on the purchase history in my Google Play account, I figured it hadn't been since about September 23, 2017. Or at least that was the last time I made an in-app purchase in BUNT.

On September 23, 2017, I purchased a "Rookie Pack Deal" for $0.99. Three days before, on September 20, 2017, I bought a "9th Inning Deal" for $9.99. And on September 15, 2017, five days before that, I bought yet another "9th Inning Deal" for $9.99. And that was far from the start of it. Going back to June 21, 2014, my shameful Google Play purchase history is full of purchases from Topps BUNT and myriad other digital trading card apps.

It all started with BUNT, Topps' digital baseball card trading app, to which I was first introduced thanks to a

June 2014 article on Beckett.com, the official website of the most prominent trading card price guide known to all humankind. At first, like with all other "FREE-mium" apps, I was perfectly happy ripping free packs of digital baseball cards using my daily log-on bonus. Sometimes I'd even go a few days without opening a pack. I'd merely log on, collect my daily coin bonus (the currency used in BUNT), trade a few baseball cards (my favorite component of the app), play in a couple low-stakes fantasy baseball-like games, and then log off. I'd occasionally rip a pack and pull an insert, which I could then flip for rarer, more desirable cards, but mostly I was content with trading cards in order to build my collection of Detroit Tigers, as well as my all-time favorite baseball player/celebrity persona since 1989, "Mr. 40/40" himself, Jose Canseco. BUNT provided me with almost all of the joy of collecting baseball cards, ripping packs, trading cards, building a personal collection, but without any of the expense or space limitations.

But clearly, I didn't remain content with the free aspect of the app for very long.

It began slowly, buying a $0.99 "Bonus Pack" here and there. But soon I realized that if you had any serious desire to collect inserts or player signatures (digital autographs on digital baseball cards), the hardest of all cards to collect, you really had no choice but to purchase additional coins. And so, buy I did.

For almost the next three years, I purchased an embarrassing number of coins from BUNT, or at least the amount is embarrassing to me. In reality, any amount spent in a digital trading card app should be embarrassing, even if it's just $0.99. But it wasn't just the in-app purchases that led me to delete BUNT from my phone. It was my obsession with BUNT, and all other digital trading card apps, that forced me to eventually swear off all digital trading cards.

Not long after I first downloaded BUNT, I also downloaded HUDDLE, the Topps football card app, which didn't take up much more of my time, because I've never been a fan of football. But what this did allow is for something the BUNT community referred to as "cross trading;" that is, organizing deals with fellow app community members in which you trade digital cards in one app for digital cards in another wholly separate app. Never mind that both apps were properties of Topps (the only current baseball card manufacturer producing MLB-licensed cards). Cross trading was explicitly forbidden from these apps, and while most cross traders were honest and relatively fair, and although baseball cards were typically seen as more valuable than football, or any other type of digital trading card, you always ran the risk of running across scammers, or members who agree to a cross trade, accept the cards they want on one app, and then deny or ignore the trade that would benefit you. Being that cross trading was not allowed in these apps, in the first place, it meant that there was no real consequence for such actions. You could complain and call names in the comment section of the apps, which occurred rather frequently, but it typically accomplished little more than possibly earning a suspension (temporary) or ban (permanent) from said app, especially if the scorned member resorted to curse words, although most were automatically censored within the app (even creative spellings of swear words were flagged).

Well, in my case, along with who knows how many members of the BUNT community, downloading BUNT was a gateway to HUDDLE (football), which led to KICK (soccer), which led to Star Wars Card

Trader, which led to KNOCKOUT (UFC), which led to The Walking Dead Card Trader, which led to SLAM (WWE), an app that miraculously featured digital autographs of long-deceased professional wrestlers, such as Andre the Giant and "Macho Man" Randy Savage. But these were only the Topps licensed digital trading card apps. I also downloaded Kitty Cards and Trump Cards, which were, as you probably guessed, digital trading cards of kittens (aww) and Donald Trump (gag), along with the other 2016 presidential candidates. I rather quickly lost interest in just about all of these apps, with the exception of BUNT and SLAM, but still, I kept up with the other apps in order to make cross trades for BUNT and SLAM.

I even had duplicate or "alt" accounts for several of the apps, which were basically dummy accounts used for hoarding and "harvesting" coins (also prohibited in the app terms and conditions). So, in addition to maintaining my primary app accounts, I would open my alt accounts, hoard coins from the daily log-on bonus, rip packs, and if I pulled an insert, trade it to my main account. And yes, of course that eventually led to purchasing coins in my alt accounts, as well, because spenders receive VIP perks, including "free" bonus cards which I could then trade for other cards I actually wanted (like Cansecos). But my spending didn't stop there.

Not only did I purchase physical Topps baseball cards, which were packaged along with randomly inserted BUNT promotional codes, but I occasionally resorted to the most shameful of all digital trading card app practices, and actually bought digital cards on eBay.

In addition to cross trading, alt accounts, and harvesting coins, buying and selling digital cards on a third-party platform like eBay was strictly prohibited, and could result in the suspension or ban of either the seller or buyer of these cards, and not unlike cross trading, buyers of digital cards were also vulnerable to scamming. But at least in the case of eBay, if a buyer did ever get scammed, eBay would hold the seller accountable, to the best of their abilities. BUNT, however, would look the other way ... unless they just decided to ban you.

I never got suspended or banned from BUNT or any other digital trading card app. I was always a friendly and enthusiastic member. If anything, I was too enthusiastic.

I never calculated exactly how much money I spent on trading card apps like BUNT and SLAM, and I can't bring myself to do it right here and now (because then I would have no choice but to publish my grand total for all to see), but I would easily estimate that it was in the hundreds. Granted, a few hundred dollars over the span of three years might not seem like much to spend on a hobby/obsession. I mean, many people spend a few hundred dollars on tangible, print baseball cards (if not one card) in a single day. But my spending habits were something I kept hidden from my family. My partner would often see me on my phone and tablet—I had separate accounts on both—playing around with my line-ups and ripping packs in BUNT and tease me about how much time I spent on there, but she had no idea (until now) that I was spending money, real money, our money, on digital trading cards, and she truly had no idea how much time I was spending on those apps.

And that—not only the money, but the time and deception behind it all—was ultimately what convinced me to swear off BUNT.

Swear it off, that is, until the night of July 28, 2019.

What can I say? The Detroit Tigers were the worst team in baseball, local sports radio was full of talk of the looming trade deadline, and in a moment of weakness/ late night boredom, my curiosity got the best of me. I wanted to see what BUNT 2019 looked like (I had successfully skipped 2018 altogether). I wanted to see if I could still access my collection. I wanted to see my precious, pristine Cansecos. So, I downloaded BUNT, and for the first time in almost two years, I opened the app.

Hey, I had 44,000 coins left in my account!

This was likely my way of leaving a little something stashed away in the off chance that I ever came back to the app, so I immediately started ripping packs. I told myself that I'd only keep the app on my phone for as long as it took me to write this essay, but my 44,000 coins were long gone before I finished a first draft, and there were so many new Cansecos to add to my collection.

# Nashville Shirt

I bought a western shirt in Nashville I now refer to as my "Nashville shirt," because it's so resplendently ugly it should only be worn in Nashville, but I've taken to wearing it in Detroit, because Detroit can appreciate an ugly shirt, too.

Our last night in Nashville, outside the hotel, there was a highly intoxicated woman in an NSYNC t-shirt. "I ain't got no shame," she was saying to the doorman. "I like to party." The next morning, we saw her at the hotel continental breakfast, clearly drunk from the night before, and still in her NSYNC t-shirt, but silent now, and stuffing her mouth with scrambled eggs.

On the drive home, from Nashville to Detroit, we paused at a truck stop in Lebanon Junction, Kentucky, where I saw a t-shirt that read *I'VE BEEN HAULIN' SINCE YOU'VE BEEN CRAWLIN'*, and I desperately wanted to buy it, but didn't feel like I earned it, having never been a long-haul trucker, just an adjunct writing instructor turned academic librarian who drives 140 miles per day to work and back.

My first day back to work, at a library in Flint, Michigan, I proudly wore my Nashville shirt, but no one commented or asked about it, good or bad, which made me think it was probably even more ugly than I originally thought.

# TGIF

I sat in my car eating egg salad while my colleagues and coworkers returned from lunch, drunk with laughter and bellies full of sushi or tacos or pizza.

I convinced myself that I had no interest in their reverie, but I wasn't invited in the first place.

*

I sat in my car eating chicken salad while students milled about in the parking lot, discussing their classes and homework.

They're undoubtedly smarter than me, future engineers and innovators, but when I overhear them swearing and complaining about professors and see them vaping cotton candy e-juice and riding longboards, I'm reminded they're the same age as my daughter, and hence I'm old enough to be their dad.

*

I sat in my car eating a handful of pistachios while two maintenance employees smoked cigarettes behind the dumpster.

*

I sat in my car eating cold meatballs while I watched a family who live across the street.

The woman arranged a load of wet laundry upon her porch and simultaneously wrangled a crew of children as the man shared a joint with the driver of a white minivan idling in their gravel driveway.

It was scorching hot, and everyone across the street was in a state of joyous undress, regardless of their body mass index or questionable choice of tattoos, and in that moment, I wanted nothing more than to strip off my sweat-dampened shirt and ask for a hit of that joint.

*

I sat in my car eating braunschweiger and onions, crying as I listened to Shania Twain's "Still the One," thinking to myself, *Thank God It's Friday*.

## When a Woman in the Taco Bell Drive-Thru Gets Out of Her Car to Pay for Her Order Because Her Driver's Side Window Doesn't Roll Down, I'm Reminded of my Mother, Rhonda

When Bruce Willis (as John McClane in *Die Hard*) pulls broken shards of glass out of his bloody bare feet, I'm reminded of my mother, Rhonda. Heart's *Bad Animals* album (on cassette) reminds me of my mother, Rhonda. Wigs and hair extensions remind me of my mother, Rhonda. Antiques remind me of my mother, Rhonda. Eating chili dogs on Halloween reminds me of my mother, Rhonda. Threatening to throw hot bacon grease in someone's face reminds me of my mother, Rhonda. Obsession by Calvin Klein reminds me of my mother, Rhonda. Handwritten letters that smell like patchouli and birthday cards that smell like patchouli and Christmas cards that smell like patchouli remind me of my mother, Rhonda. The Flarp! ™ display at Dollar Tree reminds me of my mother, Rhonda. The music video for "All I Wanna Do Is Make Love To You" by Heart, "Open Arms" by Journey, and "Don't

Cha" by The Pussycat Dolls remind me of my mother, Rhonda. Florida Georgia Line remind me of my mother, Rhonda. *Glitter* (the 2001 Mariah Carey film), as well as glitter (the sparkly material), reminds me of my mother, Rhonda. Ads for Miss Cleo and unpaid phone bills remind me of my mother, Rhonda. Slippery nipples (the shot/cocktail) remind me of my mother, Rhonda. ShopKo (northside) reminds me of my mother, Rhonda. Gallstones and gastric bypass surgery and diet pills and caffeine pills and ephedrine and "TrimSpa, baby!" and GERD and Tums and root canals all remind me of my mother, Rhonda. Drive-in theaters remind me of my mother, Rhonda. Voice-to-text, emojis, and typos remind me of my mother, Rhonda. Doilies remind me of my mother, Rhonda. There's an incomplete and ever-growing list of things that remind me of my mother, Rhonda, but more than anything else, when I'm in the Taco Bell drive-thru and have to get out of my car to pay for my shredded chicken quesaritos because my driver's side window doesn't roll down, I'm reminded of my mother, Rhonda.

# At the Drive-In

I told my mom that Katie and I were at the drive-in, and she had plenty of romantic advice to give. "Buy her some popcorn, put your arm around her shoulder, hold her hand, and kiss her on the cheek," she told me, as though this was our first date, and Katie and I hadn't been together for over eighteen years, and raised two kids and a dog. I read my mom's text to Katie, and she sarcastically gave me the finger.

"Do you remember when you took me to *American Werewolf in London?*" I asked my mom, and she immediately began to apologize. When I was about two-and-a-half years old, my mom took me to the drive-in theatre, with her then boyfriend/friend who was a boy, to see John Landis' *American Werewolf in London.* I was obviously too scared to watch the whole movie, and almost immediately began to cry at the sight of Rick Baker's groundbreaking, Academy-Award-winning horror effects, but it was one of the most formative memories of my childhood, and likely why I'm such a horror fanatic to this day. "Your grandparents weren't always so perfect," my mom said, attempting to change the subject. "They took me to the drive-in to see *The Graduate* when I was seven years old," she said. She said watching the love scenes in the car with her parents was one of the most embarrassing experiences of her life, and she still hates Dustin Hoffman for that very reason. "That's great," I said, "you should ask grandma about that," and once again the texts began to pour in. "You can never do that!" she said. "Grandma would be so mad. She would deny it. Don't ask her about it. Promise me you won't ask!" she begged via voice-to-text, and I promised her I wouldn't ask.

"What a shame," I said to Katie, "to be almost sixty years old and still not feel comfortable talking to your only living parent like an adult. Remember when Jackson puked at the drive-in?" I suddenly recalled. Our son was barely one year old, and we had taken him and his then six-year-old sister to the drive-in theatre to watch *Charlie and the Chocolate Factory*. Katie had just finished feeding Jackson a bottle—he had just recently stopped nursing—and when she sat him up on her lap, to be burped, his entire stomach full of breast milk emptied onto the dashboard. Perhaps needless to say, we didn't stick around to watch Johnny Depp's performance as Willy

Wonka, with Katie and Jackson soaked in hot, curdled breast milk, and his sister, Gabriella, throwing a crying fit over having to leave the movie early.

Well, on the night of July 3, 2020, Katie and I didn't have any kids with us at the drive-in. It was just her and me, our first movie together, alone, in god knows how long. It didn't even really matter what movie was playing, it was just good to be out of the house. "In the car, but out the house," Katie posted on Facebook. All around us, even while the movie played, thunderous fireworks lit up the horizon. "Next time we'll bring booze," we promised each other, and sighed in relief when the credits rolled, and it came time to crank the air conditioner.

# Pet Cemetery

I used to joke it was a bad omen when there was smoke rising from the chimney of the emergency veterinary clinic. One time I said this to the wrong person, forgetting her horse had recently died, and she left the library to cry in the bathroom. I couldn't fathom the amount of fire it must require to cremate a horse. After I switched jobs, I no longer drove past the smoking chimney of the emergency veterinary clinic in Flint, Michigan, and instead, my new commute took me down Evergreen Road, in Detroit. I soon came to refer to Evergreen as a pet cemetery, except it wasn't where pets were laid to rest, it was where they were slaughtered. On a regular basis, the road was littered with fresh pet carcasses. Cats mostly, but one morning, while the sun was still rising, I saw a sizable, furry mass in the middle of the road. It's voluminous coat was unmistakably golden, and my stomach knotted. "Oh ... no," I groaned. I wish I could say it looked like it was peacefully sleeping, but it didn't, and it wasn't, and so I won't. This vision haunted me for the rest of my day. I seriously considered not taking Evergreen Road into work any longer, but after I clocked out, I couldn't help driving back home the same way. I had to check if the body had been cleared from the road. I wish I could say.

# Come and Get Me

Katie's elderly aunt slept in the sun while her dad recited Red Fox punchlines, trying but failing to keep his voice down, although the remainder of the partygoers, resentfully sober Seventh-day Adventists, retreated from the heat into the house where a gray bearded man in rainbow suspenders twisted up a miniature zoo of balloon animals. I couldn't tell if it was the beer, the sun, or the air of religious judgment, but I began to feel dizzy. I tasted metal. There was a buzzing in my ear and my head felt like it was full of cotton. I caught a whiff of hot maple syrup, then putrefying garbage, both from an unknown source. Katie's dad's topic of conversation shifted from Red Fox to Rudy Ray Moore. I excused myself from the table. I opened the sliding glass door and was hit in the face with a delicious gust of cool, dry air, as well as a burst of excited voices. Sitting crosslegged in a semi-circle, children squealed in delight as the balloon man manipulated his cache of multi-colored latex, while the adults focused on gossip. I located the bathroom, closed and locked the door, and splashed cold water on my face and neck. I rinsed my mouth with water from the bathroom faucet. I could hear the screams and laughter and electricity of the party on the other side of the door. I didn't want to go back out there to all of those faces and mouths and teeth, all of those ears and eyes. I flicked off the light, sat with my back to the AC vent, and decided to take a nap. If they wanted me, they would have to come and get me.

# Trunk Sale

I couldn't recall ever being so psyched about a sign advertising a "trunk sale." I had witnessed the occasional rogue garage sale during the past year of quarantine, but all of the larger, collective sales had been cancelled, until now. The Old Village Yard and Trunk Sale was back. It was the latest in a string of returning public events, including the monthly Knights of Columbus Toy and Comic Show and the annual City of Plymouth Spring Cleanup.

The day before Spring Cleanup, everyone had a year's worth of garbage and unwanted furniture and appliances in front of their homes and a parade of vehicles rolled through the streets with drivers stopping, browsing, and collecting what they pleased. Our neighbors were unusually festive, laughter and charcoal smoke filled the air, and having finished my own bout of spring cleaning before the descent of the masses, I took some time to sit in the sun and observe. It seemed as though everyone had a pick-up, and it wasn't long before one of these pick-ups stopped in front of my house and a grizzled old man stepped out to sift through the refuse I had thrown to the curb.

"How's it going?" I said, but he did not answer. Thinking, perhaps, that he had not heard me, I called out to him again. "How are you, sir?" I said, but was ignored, and after that, I decided to keep to myself.

Growing up, my favorite day of the year wasn't Christmas or my birthday, it was my grandparents' neighborhood rummage sale. I loved searching through piles of my grandparents' neighbors' stuff, sometimes selling my own stuff and making a few bucks, and then turning around and spending it at someone else's rummage sale. I only recently realized this primed me for my love of flea markets and comic cons and book fairs, all of which were cancelled during the pandemic, and I missed them more than just about anything else, other than not seeing my mom and grandma for over one whole year.

In the absence of live entertainment and my beloved pop culture conventions and book festivals, my online shopping habits exploded. My Garbage Pail Kids collection rapidly expanded, I started buying packs of basketball cards again, I found myself scouring eBay for missing entries in my growing archive of vintage prism vending machine stickers. I often joked to my partner that I was investing in our family's future, but really, in addition to wallowing in nostalgia and attempting to recapture my lost youth, I was just keeping myself entertained, because there was little else to do, besides get drunk and play Red Dead Redemption 2, which I did a lot.

As it turns out, I wasn't the only one spending my disposable income on trading cards and stickers and comic books, and the value of many of my previous purchases went through the roof. I started perusing Beckett online price guides and watching "comps," or completed eBay sales, for items I owned, and marveled as values tripled and quadrupled. Much of this was sheer dumb luck, but I feigned like I had been a wise speculator. The only thing was, I knew I would never turn a profit, because I would never actually sell my comics and cards. That had never been the point.

I didn't hold on to my childhood Jose Canseco collection because I actually believed it would eventually fund my daughter's college education, just like I didn't start buying 1980s WWF and Garbage Pail Kids stickers because I thought I could flip them and buy a car for my son. But now, devoid of any wealth or actual assets, I have a collection that might serve as a decent little inheritance, something my kids can remember me by after I'm dead, or a cumbersome inconvenience, depending on how they feel about all of my random, ephemeral shit.

I only recently realized that I'm more or less doing the same thing as my mom, who texted me this wholly unexpected sliver of self-awareness: "Gramma cooks to show you her love and your mom makes and collects and writes and saves stuff like mementos and gifts and things from you being a baby and from your childhood to preserve special precious memories so that when I'm gone you will have all of that to remember me by."

The more I thought about it, the more it resonated with me. My boxes and binders of cards, my shelves of comics and books, my computer full of poems and essays. My collections might be more organized than my mom's, but there was little-to-no difference in their personal significance.

With this in mind, I sent a text to my daughter and son: "What would you rather inherit after I die, my comic books or my Garbage Pail Kids and baseball cards?"

Sure, they were only twenty-two and sixteen years old, but it was something I had been thinking a lot about lately, and I like to be prepared for the inevitable, when possible.

My daughter was the first to respond, "I'd appreciate not getting these texts when you are freaking 42, please … but Garbage Pail Kids," and my son predictably replied with a hyper-surreal, inappropriate meme, sans comment, so that settled it, and three weeks later when I walked to the Old Village Yard and Trunk Sale, I attended with a plan to diversify their inheritance.

# Wild Berries

While walking my dog to the "good pooping grass," as Katie and I call it, adjacent to the Plymouth Cultural Center parking lot, I passed an old man smoking a cigarette and picking wild berries. He dropped each berry in a five-gallon bucket nestled in the basket of a shopping cart he kept hidden behind a row of orange construction barrels. I wanted to get close enough to see exactly what he was picking, but I left him to his harvest undisturbed, pretended I didn't see him, and kept on walking my dog. The very next morning, when I walked my dog back to the good pooping grass, the old man wasn't there, and neither was his shopping cart or bucket, but some berries remained on the bush. Small, dense, purple wild berries. *Edible or noxious?* I asked myself as I rolled one around inside my mouth, tasting the smooth, cool, slightly bitter skin, reflecting on the old man's decision to leave the berry ripening on the branch.

# Reflux

Earlier in the evening I sent my mother a picture of my dinner, a grilled New York strip, topped with sauteed mushrooms and blue cheese crumbles, on a bed of spring greens, with a side of rosemary garlic potatoes, something I didn't do with anyone but her, but food was one of the primary points of conversation between her and my grandmother and I, something we could talk about endlessly, and peacefully, with joy, but here I was looking at that same dinner, masticated and regurgitated into a shallow plastic bowl while I sat in anguish in an Emergency Room. The pain in my gut was excruciating, an easy ten out of ten, and I sweated and writhed and paced as I tried my best to politely answer every one of the nurse's and doctor's questions. My blood pressure was high - 164/99 - but my other vitals were more or less normal. The EKG didn't show anything worthy of concern, but then again, it didn't last time, and I assumed that the x-rays I would surely have next wouldn't show anything either.

This wasn't my first trip to the Emergency Room due to wrenching abdominal pain. It had happened once before, almost exactly one year prior, over Memorial Day weekend 2020. The first time it happened, they sent me home with a diagnosis of acid reflux and a prescription for Pepcid, but not without a brief comment that sent me into a panic before I was discharged. The ER doc nonchalantly suggested I get the spot on my lung checked out. Well, fuck me, I thought, I went to the hospital because of the pain in my stomach and left with lung cancer. But lung cancer it was not. After a series of chest x-rays, CT scans, and a couple appointments with a cardiopulmonologist, I was diagnosed with the scars of histoplasmosis, a lung infection "caused by breathing in spores of a fungus often found in bird and bat droppings." I couldn't fathom where I would have come into direct contact with bird and bat droppings, but soil contaminated with bird and bat droppings could spread histoplasmosis, as well, so could it have been caused by my time spent digging up our backyard, or all of my years working in a library, with our stacks of books and magazines donated from dusty attics, moldy basements, and decrepit warehouses? Either way, it was a benign diagnosis and a new addition to my vocabulary.

The histoplasmosis may have been what created the calcified nodules on my lungs and lymph nodes, but it wasn't the cause of the pain in my gut, either then or now. According to the medical professionals, the pain was caused by my diet, or my body's reaction to my diet. Tonight, it was the steak and garlicky potatoes and blue cheese I devoured at dinner, but it was also the mango-pineapple hard seltzers and the Tito's vodka with Diet Squirt I washed it down with, as well as the half of a pepperoni Tombstone pizza I ate for lunch, and the two pamplemousse LaCroixs I drank with lunch, and the numerous cups of black coffee I drank before noon. It was my lack of ability to enjoy in moderation and my unwillingness to adjust when my body first began to show signs of revolt. Not unlike my mother before me, having her stomach stapled in her mid-twenties—a then-experimental and extreme way to reduce weight—yet still choosing to eat whatever she wanted and vomiting after every meal, I refused to take heed when doctors told me the pain I suffered could be avoided if I controlled my diet, exercised, and medicated as prescribed. Instead, I convinced myself that the diagnosis was incorrect, and continued to eat and drink more than my fill, and wound up in the Emergency Room, yet again, begging to be put out of my misery.

They responded with an injection of Haldol, an antipsy-chotic used to treat schizophrenia that is sometimes ad-ministered in the Emergency Room, instead of opioids, to treat unspecified abdominal pain. When the doctor told me this, I asked myself, do they actually believe Haldol controls pain or do they just think I'm fucking crazy, and based upon the lack of effect it had on my pain, I decided it must have been the latter. Clenching and tensing through waves of agony, I could smell my dinner in my clothes and my sweat, on my skin and es-pecially on my breath, rank, oily burps trapped in the cloth mask over my nose and mouth. Charcoal smoke and grilled beef and garlic and blue cheese, "one of my favorite combinations," I said to my mom via text after I sent the picture of my "black and blue salad," and she replied, "Holy buckets, that looks delicious!"

My mom loved to eat, but due to her stomach stapling three decades ago, she couldn't do it, or at least she couldn't do it to her liking, so instead of substantive, well-balanced, and appropriately portioned meals, she subsisted on high-sugar blended coffee drinks, gas sta-tion diet pills, and tongue-blistering flavor combinations like her most recent snack of preference, Buffalo Wing Cheez-Its crackers seasoned with granulated sugar and pecans. My mom always battled with her body image, just like myself, just like almost everyone in my mostly obese family, to whom the greatest compliment you can give is to ask, "Did you lose weight?," so she got her stomach stapled when she was less than thirty years old, and almost immediately regretted it. She found it impossible to adjust to the new restrictions on her diet, and she was horrified by the thick new pink scar that bisected her belly, so instead of eating less, she ate what she wanted and induced vomiting after every meal. She's been doing it for over thirty years now. She's a functioning bulimic, but it destroyed her teeth and her esophagus. She suffers from GERD and acid reflux. She's severely anemic. She claims that she receives blood transfusions every three to four months, due to low hemoglobin, which she tests with a take home device. To think that she's worked in health care for so many years is somewhat ironic, because she refuses to take proper care of herself. And my grandmother blames my stepdad for all of this.

My stepdad, my grandmother seethes, who showed up to my grandparents' house in a suit and tie and proposed to my mom after dating her for two weeks and took her and me away from my grandparents' home when she was twenty-one years old, and I was three. My stepdad, who became obsessed with my mother's increasing weight after she gave birth to my brother and allegedly insisted she volunteer for free, experimental stomach stapling surgery. My stepdad, who I haven't spoken to in over 25 years, and with whom my mom only occasionally communicates, since their toxic divorce, in consideration of the one and only child they conceived together.

My brother is the one who told me about my mother's alleged blood transfusions, and I flat out didn't believe him when he told me, not because I don't trust him, per se, but because this information came from our mother. So, I asked our younger sister about the blood transfusions, as well as my mother herself, and they all claimed she was receiving them, because of her advanced anemia and low hemoglobin, but still, I didn't completely believe them, and I don't know if I ever would, unless I saw, with my very own eyes, my mother being transfused with a pint of blood. I don't like that I don't/can't believe what my mother says, or what she tells other people to say on her behalf, but I've grown accustomed to it. I've come to expect it. Like Bruce Hornsby and Tupac Shakur both said, "That's just the way it is."

It was months before I told my mother about my first trip to the ER, one year ago, and how I was diagnosed with acid reflux. I wanted to make sure everything else had been eliminated before I cleared the air, but she could sympathize with the diagnosis, and she had no shortage of suggestions for how to manage it, ranging from TUMs and Rolaids to Bailey's and vanilla ice cream. But now that it's happened again, I might just keep it to myself, and hope that she doesn't ask. And as for my dinner of steak and potatoes and mushrooms and blue cheese crumbles, I won't tell her it ended up in a plastic bowl in the ER, while Katie and our son used the leftovers the following day to make chopped steak grilled cheese sandwiches, but if anybody can empathize with the tragedy of throwing up a delicious, overindulgent dinner, it's my mother.

# Toilet Humor

Katie said if they made an action figure of me it would come with a toilet auger, like how the Toxic Avenger came packaged with his mop, and this filled me with great pride. I had only purchased the toilet auger the day before, in an attempt to avoid hiring a plumber to simply unclog our toilet, but it's sturdy red handles felt so natural in my grip, and I felt a tremendous sense of satisfaction as I snaked the metal coil into the unseen depths of the brimming toilet, penetrated the soft blockage (as the auger directions called it), and flushed. "Best $30 we ever spent," I beamed, and thought maybe I entered the wrong line of work. I loved being a librarian and all, but was there anything as purely satisfying as unclogging a toilet? I mean, it was too late to actually become a licensed plumber, but maybe I could just unclog toilets on the side, me and my trusty auger. It was something I had done for previous jobs, whether or not it was my primary responsibility. When I worked at McDonald's, when I was a dishwasher at Baker's Square, even when I managed a Family Video. Many times, I had been paid to unclog toilets. I was good at it, too, with years of hands-on experience, and many of my coworkers would simply refuse to do it. So how much could I make, unclogging toilets for $10 or $20 a pop? I had even recently dreamed about unclogging a toilet. In this dream, I had driven to Wisconsin, to visit my family for the first time in over a year and ended up at a friend's apartment instead. He was sick, weak, in recovery, and he needed my help unclogging his toilet, so after I gave him a belated birthday present of a 1989 Donruss Ken Griffey Jr. Rated Rookie card, I began to ineffectually plunge away while he watched in disapproval. If I had only had my toilet auger with me, I now thought, lucid and awake, I would've cut through that muddy clog in an instant, but this dream took place weeks before we made the purchase, and so I was unsuited for the job, with just a pathetic toilet plunger in hand.

# 72 Hours

I watched in awe as my mom spent $250 on thrift shop costume jewelry, and a vintage glass owl for my sister. She offered to buy me anything I wanted in the store, but the only thing I chose was a Donny Wahlberg New Kids on the Block button, for Katie. I didn't tell her about the clown painting I was eyeing, as she tried on assorted sterling silver rings. My mom took the NKOTB button and said, "Aw, your grandma always says your grandpa looked like him." "She thinks grandpa looked like Donny Wahlberg?" I said, and she said, "No, James Dean," and I explained that the man on the button was Donny Wahlberg (Marky Mark's brother), not James Dean. "Katie believes Donny is the superior Wahlberg," I said to my mom, and the cashier/owner of the thrift shop, a loyal fan of *Blue Bloods*, whole-heartedly agreed.

Later that afternoon, I watched in similar awe as my mom filled her arms at a convenience store. She'd had a sudden, insatiable craving for Munchos, but she walked out of the store with Munchos, Planters Cheez Balls, another bag of organic air-popped cheese balls, Tostitos cheese dip, a Hershey's chocolate bar with almonds, and a 20-ounce bottle of Baja Blast. She ate a little of it all, took one drink of the Baja Blast, and threw the rest in the garbage.

The following day, when her departing flight was delayed, she began texting me and my three siblings. She insisted that she was starving, and she wanted to go home. She begged me to come back and pick her up from the airport, luggage be damned. She was ready to walk away from everything she had brought with her on vacation, including the costume jewelry and owl she just bought at the thrift shop. The suitcase wasn't even hers, it was borrowed from my grandma, but she didn't care. She'd leave it behind in a heartbeat. She said she could buy a new suitcase and replace everything in it. She said she would've felt better if I let her bring some ricotta cheese to the airport. I lost track of how many times I told her she wasn't allowed to bring an open tub of ricotta through security, but for all intents and purposes, this might as well have been the first time. Ricotta, cottage cheese, peanut butter, vanilla ice cream, Mtn Dew, and Chocolate Therapy Ben and Jerry's: those were her requests when I asked if there was any food she needed for her weekend visit, being well aware of her various dietary "eccentricities," and most of it now sat, barely touched, in my refrigerator/freezer.

After my mom's flight finally departed, I set to cleaning our kitchen, bathroom, and my office, where she slept on our pullout couch for the past three nights. I quickly filled a garbage bag with partially eaten food and amassed a collection of half-empty bottles and cans. I swept up a small pile of dropped and discarded pills and prayed that our dog hadn't eaten any of them. Surely he had enjoyed the fruits of my mom's frequent spillage, a result of her failing eyesight caused by a once detached retina, and he was going to miss licking her salty, sunbaked feet.

# Blood Bait

My 83-year-old grandmother is having a recurring dream. In my grandmother's dream, her grandchildren are toddlers again, and they're running away from her. Every night, she hears one of her grandchildren running through her house, but she can't find them, and she can't catch them. Myself, my brother, my eldest cousin. I'm curious how long it will continue. Will she dream about all eight of her adult grandchildren, and then her five great grandchildren, as well? My grandmother's house is almost empty. There's no more kids or grandkids living with her, living off of her. It's just her in there, my grandfather dead for ten years. She talks a lot about what's going to happen to her house when she's gone, how much it might sell for, and what her kids might do with the money. She worries that my mother will squander her share. One of her oldest neighbors died last year, and his house was gutted and put up for sale. I couldn't resist the curiosity of seeing what the inside of his house looked like, being years since I last stepped inside, so my partner and I hopped on Zillow and scrolled through the slideshow of his empty ranch. His youngest son was one of my closest childhood friends, but I haven't seen or talked to him in nearly twenty years. I heard he married a woman from the Philippines and broke his back in a snowboarding accident, but I knew little else about his life. There were years when he and I were inseparable, or perhaps it was more that I had clung to his side. He was two years older than me, but only one grade ahead, because he was held back in kindergarten. I still have a scar above my lip, on the left side of my mouth, from when he accidentally hit me with a snow shovel. He was the person who introduced me to *Monty Python and the Holy Grail,* and he suggested that I read Hemingway's *The Old Man and the Sea.* He was from a family of hunters and fishers, we all were where I grew up in Wisconsin, but his family did little else but hunt and fish. Their deep freeze was stocked with venison, their house was decorated with antlers and pelts and taxidermied bass, and their backyard was often littered with the carcasses of snapping turtles. My friend sold furs to the local trading company, and he applied for his commercial fishing license as soon as he was old enough to legally do so. He occasionally invited me to help check his lines or bait his hooks, and I dutifully obliged. My friend left buckets of blood on his deck. He bought blood from the butcher, or he harvested it from the animals he hunted, and he allowed the blood to congeal in the sun, where it turned to stinking, rotting jelly, and we used it to bait his lines. I enjoyed the process of baiting his lines with homemade blood bait, plunging my hand into the bucket, my knife easily slicing off gelatinous pieces of congealed blood, ignoring the white maggots writhing on the deep red meniscus. One afternoon, after returning from the lake, he made us lunch, a frozen pepperoni pizza. We were the only two in his house, so he popped a video in the living room VCR - *Gazongas 2* - the first pornographic movie I ever saw, and we watched it while eating our pizza. I remembered all of this, and more, while Katie and I perused my friend's dad's house on Zillow. We both agreed that it was overpriced. I couldn't help thinking it might not be long before pictures of my grandmother's empty house would be on Zillow, and people will probably think it's overpriced too.

# Deer Meat

I broke my ankle on Super Bowl Sunday because I slipped on the ice in my driveway while bringing in the groceries and bidding on wrestling cards on my phone at the same time. It was an embarrassing accident, to say the least, one that kept me at home on the couch, unable to drive myself to work, make dinner, or go up and down the stairs by myself.

I hadn't left the house in over a week, until my partner took pity on me and drove me around our neighborhood like an old, wounded dog about to get put to sleep. Our mailman saw me as I struggled to get out of the car, comically large orthopedic boot on my right leg, crutches wedged in my armpits.

"Are you ok?" he asked. I told him I broke my ankle and the mailman told me that Joe Rogan recommends I eat deer meat. "Lots of deer meat," he said, "because deer are fast and have more protein," unlike slovenly pigs and cows, he added, and eating deer meat would heal my broken bone faster. He claimed he once had a broken hand that his doctor told him would take six months to heal, but he ate lots of deer meat and was better in three, then he told me which of my neighbors had ring cameras, and which would be easier to have packages stolen off their porch.

"Thanks, I'll try the venison," I said, tucking away his suggestion to rip-off my neighbors, and was reminded of my mother, who treated her bulimia-induced anemia by eating liverwurst and braunschweiger sandwiches (for the iron, of course). I hadn't gone deer hunting since I was sixteen and I wasn't sure I could even find deer meat where I lived, aside from fetid piles of roadkill or the occasional bag of venison jerky, but I suddenly had a craving for succulent, milk-fed veal.

When I was a kid, my favorite food was veal parmesan, so rich and morally dubious, but I never had it home-made, despite my mother's Italian roots. Every once in a while, my mom would splurge and buy a tray of frozen Stouffer's Veal Parmigiana, and it made any meal feel like a bacchanal.

One time, my step-grandparents took me and my little brother out for lunch at Country Kitchen and told us we could order anything we wanted on the menu. My step-grandparents ordered ribeye steak and onions, well done, with pools of Hunt's ketchup, my brother chicken tenders, and I, the adopted bastard, didn't hesitate to order the veal parmesan. Upon hearing my order, my Scandinavian step-grandmother scanned the laminated menu and recoiled, "The most expensive thing on the menu," and my fat face burned with shame.

"I'm not cooking venison," my partner said as she helped me hobble up the stairs, and I asked, "Do you think Stouffer's still makes a veal parmesan?"

# Beer and Sushi

One of my son's friends was working the register when I stopped to buy gas station sushi and a six-pack of Molson.

Last time I saw him, in fall of 2019, I took him and my son to Tyler, the Creator at the Masonic Temple, so I didn't recognize him now with his curly black mullet and matching mustache.

I'm sure plenty of his friends' parents stroll through his line, but I wondered how many of them had taken him to a concert in Detroit when he was 15, and if I was the first on a Saturday night, buying beer and sushi in a Dusty Rhodes t-shirt?

I paid and stepped outside as a woman whipped down the street on an ATV with a toddler on back—no shoes, no helmet, no baby seat, just a toddler holding on for dear life.

And they were fucking glorious.

# Virgil, Virgil, Virgil
*Rest in Peace*

Virgil was the first professional wrestler I ever paid to meet. He was a guest at the Motor City Comic Con in May 2012, and I paid him to sign a glossy color copy of the cover of the January 1988 *WWF Magazine* featuring him and the Million Dollar Man Ted DiBiase, and then I took a picture with him, our fists interlocked, while I held the gold-plated, cubic zirconia encrusted Million Dollar Championship belt. I mentioned that I saw him wrestle live once, in my hometown of LaCrosse, Wisconsin, and he said, "LaCrosse, Wisconsin … Colder than a motherfucker, right? I remember that shit," and then we parted ways.

I met Virgil a second time a little less than one year later, in March 2013, at Heroes and Legends Wrestling in Fort Wayne, Indiana, my first independent wrestling show and fan convention since I became interested in pro wrestling again, as an adult. I did not give Virgil any money that day, even though he insisted, almost demanded, that I pay him to take a selfie with him or have him sign an autograph. Instead, I paid for meet and greets with Koko B. Ware and Colt Cabana, but I felt like I spent nearly as much time socializing with Virgil, wandering the fan convention, and lounging at the bar above the covered ice rink used for the venue, as I did with the friend who drove with me the two and a half hours to Fort Wayne.

Neither of these times did I mention to Virgil that he was the first professional wrestler I ever shook hands with. I figured that might have been a little too personal and off-putting, and reserved that detail for myself. But it was true. Virgil was the first professional wrestler I ever touched. I was at a WWF house show with my brother and stepdad, and before Virgil made his way to the ring, in his red and white striped tights, my brother and I ran to the guard rail, like all of the kids did, like all of the kids still do, no matter who was making their entrance, and we leaned over so Virgil could slap our hand. And he did. Virgil slapped my hand, like he did with all the other kids I saw on TV. Virgil wasn't the most popular wrestler on the card that night, and in the years since, Virgil has become known more as a punchline than a professional wrestler, but since he was the first professional wrestler to ever make contact with my hand, Virgil will always hold a very special place in my memory.

It annoys me that I don't remember more about the wrestling shows I attended as a kid, and the memories I do recall barely feature the actual wrestling that took place. I remember Virgil slapping my hand, as previously mentioned, but other than that, my list of memories is short and vague. I have foggy memories of seeing Hulk Hogan and Andre the Giant. I remember seeing Nikolai Volkoff, the despised Russian heel, and I remember that as everyone in attendance at the LaCrosse Center aggressively chanted "USA, USA, USA," I thought it would be funny to chant for the USSR instead, and my stepdad smacked the back of my head for doing so. I remember leaving events early so my stepdad could beat traffic. I think I went to at least two WWF shows with just my stepdad before my brother was old enough to come with us, but I never previously thought to ask my brother if he remembered anything about this. I haven't spoken to my stepdad in nearly 25 years, so I wasn't about to call him up and ask if he remembered taking me to see the WWF, so I decided one day, on the tenth anniversary of the death of Macho Man Randy Savage, to simply ask my brother if he remembered anything about going to watch wrestling with me, and I was pleasantly surprised by his reply.

"I remember seeing Virgil," he immediately texted, and I thought it was quite funny that Virgil was the highlight of both of our nights. He said he also remembered getting a pair of Bret the Hitman Hart sunglasses from the merch stand, and I was immediately jealous, because I didn't remember ever getting a souvenir, although I later recalled being allowed to buy a yellow and red Hulk Hogan foam finger. The fact that we both remembered Virgil was a solid detail though, because if nothing else it pinpointed a specific time in Virgil's career. This was after his departure from the Million Dollar Man, his longtime in-ring "boss" and dehumanizer, after he turned babyface and went on a briefly successful singles run. Thanks to a website called *The History of WWE*, which archives the results of WWF/E shows, my brother identified that the house show we attended was on January 24, 1992. As far as my brother could find, that was the only WWF show at the LaCrosse Center where Virgil appeared as a singles wrestler after turning on DiBiase. It was a small victory, but I was so excited that he found this detail. I read the concise tally of results, and nothing felt familiar, aside from the appearance of Virgil, but I was convinced this had to be the show we attended. In January 1992, I would have been twelve years old, and my brother would have been eight, nearly nine. I would've still been a fan of wrestling, and specifically the WWF, but it would have been near the eventual decline in my interest, when my passion would have started to shift to baseball cards and other "real" sports.

Overall, the match card for this show looked pretty lackluster (Chris Walker defeats Hercules!), a rather typical house show but, on paper, the main event of Intercontinental Champion Rowdy Roddy Piper versus WWF World Champion Ric Flair looked like a real standout match. I couldn't believe I might have seen Piper and Flair locked up in a ring together and not remember it, but clearly I was more excited about in-ring performers like Virgil, Skinner, and the Berzerker, at the time, and I guess I wasn't alone in that. In a January 25, 1992 *LaCrosse Tribune* article titled "Theater in the Flesh," journalist Geri Parlin dedicates the first three paragraphs of her review of the January 24th WWF show to the Berzerker, "flaunting his Viking helmet and skimpy tunic," and later refers to the crowd, "with blood lust in their hearts and programs in their fists," chanting "Virgil, Virgil, Virgil," and barely mentions the main event between all-time greats Roddy Piper and Ric Flair, other than briefly referring to Piper pulling down Flair's tights, before losing to him via disqualification.

In May of 2015, I would meet Rowdy Roddy Piper at Motor City Comic Con, the same venue I met Virgil three years before, and where I'd eventually meet Vader and Diamond Dallas Page, as well. I didn't mention seeing Piper wrestle Ric Flair in LaCrosse, Wisconsin, because I had completely forgotten that I had ever actually seen him live, but when he asked me when it was that I saw him for the first time, I mentioned the wrestling program *Saturday Night's Main Event*. I didn't reference a specific match, but I told him my mom would occasionally wake me up on Saturday nights, after my bedtime, if *Saturday Night's Main Event* came on NBC instead of *Saturday Night Live*. Piper told me that my mom was a good woman, then we took a series of absurdly blurry pictures together while the man helping out at Piper's booth struggled to learn how to use the camera in my cell phone. Piper suddenly died two months after I met him, at the age of sixty-one, and at the news of his death, I felt immensely grateful that I had that brief opportunity to meet him, shake his hand, and thank him for his legendary body of work.

So, while Virgil may have been the first professional wrestler I ever paid to meet, he would be far from the last. I'm currently forty-two years old, and just a few weeks ago, I walked five minutes from my home to State of Comics in Plymouth, Michigan to meet AEW's TNT Champion Darby Allin, a lithe, tattooed, skateboarding wrestler with a painted face whose name is an homage to Darby Crash (of the Germs) and GG Allin. The morning of my first meet and greet in over a year, during breakfast, I sincerely asked Katie if she thought I was getting too old to pay to wait in line to meet professional wrestlers, especially those who were nearly half my age, rather than the retired legends I grew up watching, but by the time I got to my local comic shop, where Darby Allin was making his special appearance, and I saw the extended line of excited fans waiting to meet Darby, some with their faces painted like his, many holding Darby Allin action figures (mine was safely nestled "mint in box" in my backpack), others with replica championship belts over their shoulders, and almost everyone wearing wrestling t-shirts or hoodies or hats, I felt fully in my element, and confident in my decision to spend the better part of a gorgeous afternoon standing in line, waiting to meet another professional wrestler.

# Fancy Meatloaf

*for Katie*

I was simply looking for a new way to make use of the miscellaneous meats and vegetables purchased for the pandemic, but it just doesn't get any better than a frozen pepperoni pizza, eaten outdoors while playing Yahtzee, listening to Zapp & Roger, and drinking iced Rosé, after a full day of spreading cedar mulch and planting arborvitae, with the woman you've loved since 2002.

# Publication Notes

Much love to advance readers Michael Chin, Alan Good, Adam Van Winkle, and Mathias Nelson, and thanks to the editors of the publications in which versions of the following pieces first appeared.

*Back Patio Press: Spontaneous, Bed Bugs, On the 5th Anniversary of Taking My Daughter to Warped Tour 2013, At the Drive-In, Deer Meat, Nashville Shirt, Come and Get Me, Toilet Humor*

*Beer Money (Malarkey Books): TGIF*

*BULL: Beer and Sushi*

*Cowboy Jamboree Magazine: Humiliation, PWI*

*Depression Cookbook (Badlung Press): Fancy Meatloaf*

*Hobart: Bennigan's, Relisted*

*Iron Horse Literary Review: Black River*

*Kleft Jaw Press: Exquisite, I Quit*

*Misery Tourism: Pet Cemetary*

*OBSESSED: Essays on Pop Culture Obsession (Gimmick Press): To BUNT, or Not to BUNT*

*OW III: Rock Me, Roll Me, Jackyl Me Off!*

*Nobody Knows You're a Dog (Badlung Press): Low Years, Poke*

*Philosophical Idiot: Everything Zen, I Think You Loved Me More When I Used to Wear Sweatpants, Musk, Thinking About Trying to Teach Again, What She Expects Me to Do*

*Red Fez: American Stepdad, Attack at the Yack 2, In Silence, Meeting Macho, Participation Trophies, Piece by Piece, Proverbs 19:17, Raccoons Ain't Nothing to Fuck With, Things You Never Knew Existed, "The Hammer" Takes a Knee, Watch Out!, Trunk Sale, 72 Hours*

*Rejection Letters: Wild Berries, Reflux, Blood Bait*

*Slam Wrestling: Virgil, Virgil, Virgil*

*Taco Bell Quarterly, Vol. 4: When a Woman in the Taco Bell Drive-Thru Gets Out of Her Car*

Josh Olsen is a librarian, a columnist for SlamWrestling.net, and the co-creator of Gimmick Press, an independent micro publisher of pop culture inspired literature and art, including *Working Stiff: The Anthology of Professional Wrestling Literature & Art.*

# MORE ROADSIDE PRESS TITLES:

# MORE ROADSIDE PRESS TITLES:

## MORE ROADSIDE PRESS TITLES:

*Disposable Darlings*
Todd Cirillo

*Full Moon Midnight*
Belinda Subraman

*Innocent Postcards*
John Pietaro

*Cistern Latitudes*
James Duncan

*Another Saturday Night in Jukebox Hell*
Alan Catlin

*Abandoned By All Things*
Karl Koweski

*Ain't These Sorrows Sweet?*
Lauren Scharhag

*Gregory Corso: Ten Times a Poet*
Leon Horton, Editor

*She Throws Herself Forward to Stop the Fall*
Dave Newman

*We Don't Get to Write the Ending*
Aleathia Drehmer

*These Many Cold Winters of the Heart*
Ryan Quinn Flanagan

*Green Roses Bloom for Icarus*
Hiromi Yoshida

www.ingramcontent.com/pod-product-compliance
Lightning Source LLC
Chambersburg PA
CBHW020256130626
46549CB00005B/2233